Photo by Mina Whiting

JOHN O' LONDON (WILFRED WHITTEN)

THE JOY OF LONDON
AND OTHER ESSAYS

BY
JOHN O' LONDON (WILFRED WHITTEN)

Selected, and with an Introduction, by
FRANK WHITAKER

LONDON
GEORGE NEWNES LIMITED
TOWER HOUSE, SOUTHAMPTON STREET
STRAND, W.C.2

First Published . . 1943

Made and Printed in Great Britain by
Wyman & Sons, Ltd., London, Fakenham and Reading

CONTENTS

INTRODUCTION

By Frank Whitaker

WILFRED WHITTEN, whose other and better-known self was "John o' London," died on December 19, 1942, within a few months of his seventy-ninth birthday. More than fifty of those years were spent in and about Fleet Street, and his memories of Victorian London went back further still. He remembered walking, as a boy, under old Temple Bar: he lived to see the Temple itself, which he knew and loved so well, blasted into rubble by German bombs. Knife-board buses and hansom cabs were the currency of the streets when he pushed his first manuscript through the letter-box of a London newspaper, and jingle and hoof-beat the tune to which Londoners nightly went to bed. He lived to see a hansom cab stared at half-incredulously in the London Museum and to write some of his last articles in a deep air-raid shelter, with guns booming in the dark overhead. Throughout this age of feverish change he remained, in Sainte-Beuve's happy phrase, a devoted secretary of the public, critically recording the present, pensively recalling the magic of the past. Many of those who knew and loved him have expressed a wish that his "desiccated toils" should not be allowed to lie buried in forgotten files. Accordingly I offer to his memory this small collection of his essays and verses.

With one exception they were written for *T.P.'s Weekly* and *John o' London's Weekly* between the years 1903 and 1942. The exception is part of a chapter from his book *A Londoner's London*, now out of print. Owing to war-time difficulties I have been unable to cast my net as widely as I could have wished. Much of his earlier work appeared in newspapers and periodicals that no longer exist—the *Globe*, the *Academy* and Harry Furniss's *New Budget* among them.   It was often unsigned, or signed in different ways, so that getting access to their files, even had I been able to trace them, would have been only one, and not the most difficult, part of the search.   In happier days, perhaps, someone may think it worth while to cover the ground more thoroughly.   I hope someone will.   In the meantime I shall be happy if this book is regarded as a true microcosm of Whitten's unique contribution to the literary journalism of his time.   I like to think, at all events, that he himself had a hand in shaping it.   After his death were found a number of scrap-books, in which he had pasted all the articles he apparently wanted to preserve— perhaps half a million words in all.   There were my chief source of supply.

I have ventured to describe Whitten's work as unique in his generation.   How was it unique?   In the first place I know of no one of his time who stood in quite the same relation to the reading public.   One or two of his con- temporaries—Robertson Nicoll for instance, and Arnold Bennett at different stages of his career—had a bigger influence on the fortunes of books and authors, and T. P. O'Connor was a more seductive spell-binder.   But Nicoll appealed to a different public, Bennett's influence was more spasmodic, and O'Connor never seemed to find his true mission.   Whitten never doubted either his own powers or his mission.   He was neither an advocate nor a proselytiser, except in his articles on English, to which I shall refer later.   He excelled in communicating to others his own quiet enjoyment of what he had seen and read; and because he had read deeply, if not widely, because of his ability to "discern the infinite suggestiveness of common things," because of his tolerance and good taste, he attracted a considerable following and kept it to the end. "I doubt whether any writer on books in recent years," Robert Lynd has written of him, "was regarded affectionately by so large an audience. He had a rare gift for coming to terms of personal intimacy with his readers, so that as you read one of the 'John o' London' letters you felt that you were sitting on a chair and listening to the conversation of a man you liked." At one of their early meetings T. P. O'Connor impressed on him that every line in the newly conceived *T.P.'s Weekly* must "thra-arb with human int'rist." The admonition was never forgotten: human interest became Whitten's spiritual food as it had been T. P.'s. "He never suggested that any book should be read except for enjoyment," Robert Lynd goes on. "For him good writers were men to be loved rather than to be analysed. The title of a famous Victorian work, *The Friendship of Books*, suggests admirably the spirit in which he set out to be a guide through the gardens of literature." Countless people now of middle age must have owed to him their first intimate contact with good books.

He was unique, I think, for the range of his knowledge, or more exactly for his thorough grasp of an odd range of subjects—eighteenth and nineteenth-century London, Lamb and his circle, the Old Testament, mediæval York, the caves at Margate, the Shakespeare-Bacon controversy, Rembrandt's etchings and Constable's landscapes, the knotty points of English grammar. Although he owed much to Jespersen and H. W. Fowler, his feeling for good English was largely instinctive; yet it led him almost against his will into one of the chief activities of his later life. Every week for more than twenty years, over the pen-name "Jackdaw," he sparred expertly with the grammatical problems of readers of *John o' London's Weekly*. I doubt if any grammarian of his time was consulted so often: it would be hard to find one who treated such a glum subject with such unfailing freshness, good humour, and plain common sense. He was completely free from pedantry. He believed that in everyday life "good English follows clear thinking rather than that system of rules called Grammar, which youth loathes and maturity forgets." He was never tired of repeating that grammar was made for man, and not man for grammar. Sometimes he seemed to carry waywardness too far; occasionally, during the years I was in charge of *John o' London's*, I was thrown into an agony of indecision, as the paper was going to press and he was far away, by a ruling that I felt certain was wrong. I need not have worried. I came to know that behind his apparent jauntiness lay the wariness of the cat and the guile of the serpent. At precisely the right moment, when his readers were sizzling with indignation or superior knowledge, and he appeared to be without a leg to stand on, he would produce some unanswerable argument, some unimpeachable authority, and set out with a chuckle on another tack. His book *Is It Good English?* (dedicated to "Men, women and grammarians") and his share of *Good and Bad English* (in which I had the privilege of collaborating with him), illustrate the originality and clear-sightedness of his method at its best.

Finally, he can have had few rivals in the quality, regularity and extent of his output. I calculate that in the last fifty years of his working life he pencilled in his large round hand not far short of seven million words. Usually he wrote under pressure, for he never learnt to organise his time, yet his gift for turning a characteristic phrase, for recalling an apt quotation, never failed. He was indeed a master of what he liked to call, echoing the Psalmist, the craft of the Ready Writer.

*   *   *   *   *

Whitten was born in Newcastle on March 7, 1864. His family were Quakers, and his father, a prosperous tea merchant, sent him to a preparatory school at Sidcot, and in due time to those two good Quaker schools, Ackworth and Bootham. In later life his schoolboy memories seemed to centre on Ackworth; he hardly ever mentioned Bootham, although it was then, as now, the more important institution of the two. But he loved Ackworth—perhaps because he spent his more formative years there—and his recollections of it, recorded in a little book called *Between the Cupolas* published in 1905, are extraordinarily clear and detailed. The book has probably long been out of print, but it still has the power to delight a wider audience than it was intended for. I commend the passage I shall quote from it in a moment to all young people who are tempted to take up writing as a career. Even in childhood Whitten had been fond of writing. He produced a family budget called *Small Talk* when he had barely reached his teens, and when he went to Ackworth he started a more ambitious school magazine which had a merry life until it was suppressed by Authority. Later on he was awarded a guinea prize for an essay on total abstinence, written with all the weight of his fifteen years' experience behind it. Musing on these events twenty-five years later, he asks whether the triumphs achieved in school essay societies have any "prognostic relation" to a future literary career. He thinks not, and goes on:

I do not believe that the most astute critic can judge whether work done in the teens is an end or a beginning. It is a curious reflection that your crudely exuberant writing youth is often producing work equal to that done at the same age by men whose names are planetary. For a few years, and as it were contemporaneously, he is the equal of—who knows: Shakespeare himself?—but let us say of Byron, Dickens, Landor, Meredith, Maeterlinck. They increased and he may decrease, but meanwhile his work baffles inference and escapes contempt. For is it an end or a beginning? . . .

It is only when a young fellow has emerged from his youthful exercise in essay-writing, and is brought into contact with events, topics and social conditions, that you can tell whether he has the faculty of taking subjects straight from life, and the rapidity and freshness which journalism demands. The true end of an Essay Society is to produce readers, not writers. And there are thousands to whom it may not be useless to point out that he who writes for a living is of all men the most starved of good reading. In the New Grub Street there is neither time nor silence for browsing on books.

"An end or a beginning?" How neatly the phrase sums up the difficulty felt, I imagine, by all editors who are regularly confronted with the work of adolescents. In Whitten's case these early scribblings, together with a certain precocity in elocution which was long remembered by the friends of his schooldays, did as we know point to a future career, but many tedious years were to elapse before he found his feet. Meanwhile, in those impressionable years at Ackworth and Bootham, he found time to read as well as to write. At fifteen, as can be gathered from his letters to his mother, he knew his Lamb from cover to cover. It was the same with Hazlitt and Boswell. He had a passion for Disraeli. When Carlyle died, "I am so exceedingly attached to him as an author," he wrote, "that I could almost mourn him as a friend." And whatever he read he remembered, and could draw upon at a moment's notice.

From York he went back to Newcastle to join his father's tea business, but although his family relationships were always happy he found work behind the counter uncommonly dull. He wanted to write. Above all he longed to go to London. Even as a child this longing was so intense that it filled not only his waking thoughts but his dreams as well. Night after night he used to dream that he was in an express train flying towards a vast building which he recognised as St. Paul's Cathedral, with its great dome blotting out the stars. The dream did not leave him until at the age of fifteen he went south for a holiday, and was able to gaze on St. Paul's in reality.

When he was twenty-two, his father having retired, he seized the opportunity to come to London for good. His first job was in a Mincing Lane counting house, where he entered up ledgers from nine to six. He hated the ledgers, but was so thrilled by the great city that he said he was "ready to do the work of the very errand boy to get out into those streets and learn my way about them." He never forgot the ecstasy of his first taste of the joy of London. It shines through his account, written in *A Londoner's London* thirty years later, of his search for rooms:

The first perch! There was no reason why I should have chosen my own in the dismal region of Hoxton. But when I had found acceptance in the City and was, so to speak, a licensed Londoner, I had no better plan than to walk in random search of a roof. I like to remember that casual faring into London's arms. As it happened I wandered north, up Moorgate Street, past the Artillery ground, blinking with joy when I saw Finsbury Square, nobly metropolitan, and the Bunhill burial-ground—eloquent of the City's dusty past.

I walked up the New North Road without rudder, and thought that the names above the little shops of clockmakers, newsagents, and small milliners were possible only in London and in the novels of Dickens. In a side-street a decent house showed a card in its window, and in five minutes I was lord of a chamber whose window looked on the mysterious 'backs' of another street. That night I said: "These, then, are

London dwellings, and they were old before I was born."
A light would travel up some stairs, gleaming and failing
as it went up from landing to landing. Resolving to
make a unique collection of London shopkeeper's names,
I fell asleep. I have never made that collection, but I
believe that the only man in London named Oliver
Twist lives to-day in my old Hoxton.

"I hope there are still youths," he says elsewhere, "who
when they come to London, think of Troy and Bagdad and
Eldorado." I wonder if any writer of his time lured more
of them to London than John o' London himself.

He spent several years among what he called "the top-
hatty, tailor-modelled men" of Mincing Lane, who seemed
to him "incapable of so much that gives grace and vivacity
and interest to life," and then decided that he must turn
author or perish. How near he came to perishing nobody
knows, but there is evidence that he had a hard struggle.
He hawked books from door to door. He earned an
occasional guinea by writing "turn-overs"—special articles
overlapping from one page to another—for the London
papers. But he did so badly that he seriously thought of
enlisting in the Army—a fantastic thought to anybody who
knew him, for he would have been as much at home with
a rifle as a prima donna with a harpoon. However,
Quaker friends came to his assistance. He was com-
missioned to write a life of Whittier, and did it so well
that other commissions followed.

He published two slim volumes called *Quaker Pictures* and
an excellent short life of Defoe. About this time, as he tells
in one of the essays in this book, he formed a friendship with
E. V. Lucas which was to last until Lucas's death, and which
brought Whitten both happiness and profit. Although
the younger man, Lucas already moved in a wider circle
and was better endowed with worldly wisdom. He

introduced Whitten to one or two literary clubs, helped
him to find a more regular market for his freelance articles,
and generally stimulated him to greater activity. From
this point I am enabled to carry on the story by Sir John
Hammerton, who has kindly sent me the following note:

"My first meeting with Wilfred Whitten takes me back
to the end of 1900 or early in 1901. He was at that time
employed in a diversity of ways earning his living on the
London press. Among his activities had been the editorship of a journal concerned with the catering business, and
like myself at that time, he was a frequent contributor
of "turn-overs" to the old *Globe*, and paragraphist at large.
He worked also for Harry Furniss's illustrated weekly
The New Budget, with which he was earlier identified when
it was known as the *Pall Mall Budget*. It was the *Pall
Mall Budget* that first brought him into contact with Lewis
Hind. Not long afterwards Hind appointed him assistant
editor of the remodelled *Academy*, for which he wrote
reviews and personal paragraphs. Everything he wrote
had the real literary tang.

"In those days we knew each other with more than the
intimacy of mere acquaintanceship. He lived at Hatch
End, or somewhere out Pinner way, and once a week we
used to walk about the Euston Road for an hour or so after
we had dined at our literary coterie, talking earnestly about
men and books until the last trains for our northern
suburbs were about to leave. When T. P. O'Connor
decided to found *T.P.'s Weekly* he asked my dear friend
Coulson Kernahan, so recently departed, to recommend an
acting editor and he promptly nominated me, but my
commitments in Paternoster Row at that time were too
considerable. Whitten was then offered the job, and it
was a lucky day for T.P. when he secured his co-operation:
no journalist in London was better equipped to popularise
the literary life. His love of books and bookmen, and

above all his love of London, coloured his whole existence and made his companionship a joy to the privileged few who shared it in those distant days.   He was in the true succession of those who derive from Elia."

*   *   *   *   *

In his essay on T. P. O'Connor, reprinted in this book, Whitten gives us his own account of how he left the *Academy* in 1902 for the newly-founded *T.P.'s Weekly*.   He fell under T.P.'s spell at once, and although he could write that gifted Irishman's head off, he modestly referred to him ever afterwards as "my master T. P."   In fact he has never had the credit he deserved for making *T.P.'s Weekly* the most widely read literary journal of its time.   T.P. was certainly its inspiration, but Whitten did most of the work. In the paper's early days T.P. wrote a good deal of it himself, but he had so many irons in the fire that his enthusiasm soon waned.   The time came when he did not even read the books he reviewed.   Extracts were typed out for him on slips of paper by his "ghosts," and he would then dovetail them into an article so skilfully that no one could detect the joins.   He was an adept at such tricks of the trade, and as he had shown earlier when he founded the *Star*, he was also unerringly shrewd in his choice of men.   Whitten had several capable associates—J. A. T. Lloyd, C. Kennet Burrow and Reginald Buckley among them—and the business side of the paper was admirably managed by Walter Grierson, a Scotsman who later played an important part in controlling the George Newnes publications.

It was while he was with T.P. that Whitten became John o' London.   He borrowed the name from the Westminster monk and historian of the fourteenth century, more I think to satisfy his almost mystical attachment to the word London than for any other reason.   He had used it occasionally in the *Academy* days: henceforward he used it whenever he wrote at all.   It was in his early years with

T.P.'s too, that he published his first books (apart from the life of Defoe) for general circulation. *London in Song*, an anthology, was beautifully produced by Grant Richards, but it was not successful, and can now be picked up only occasionally in second-hand shops. *London Stories*, in two volumes, was intended for a more popular public, and sold well. Whitten must have put an immense amount of work into it, for it is more than a thousand pages long, and seems to contain every scrap of London lore ever recorded.*

After nine years of *T.P.'s Weekly* he decided to go back to freelance work, and handed over the acting editorship to Holbrook Jackson. The first-fruits of his freedom were new editions of J. T. Smith's *Book for a Rainy Day* and *Nollekens and His Times*, and in 1913 came his best book, *A Londoner's London*, in which he again played the guide to the hallowed ground between Hyde Park Corner and Aldgate Pump, and from Islington down to the river.

There have been many books about London, but I know of none that excels this in knowledge, enthusiasm, and what Matthew Arnold called ease of movement. It had a double purpose. It not only recalled the past: it also warned Londoners of what was disappearing under their noses. The housebreakers were unusually busy at that time, and wherever they were to be found Whitten's sharp eyes were on them, reminding us that their picks and crowbars were uprooting not only bricks and mortar, but history itself. The book was written, I believe, to appear serially in one of T.P.'s publications, and it is a pity that its sense of the moment should detract from its permanent value. But it illustrates better than any other work of Whitten's what I may call his topographical flair, his extraordinary respon-

* Some of this material was used later, in an abridged form, in two books published by Newnes under the titles *London Stories* and *More London Stories*. To the same series John o' London contributed a collection of lost-and-found quotations entitled *Treasure Trove*.

siveness to the aura of a place. Indeed, his affection for London, and later on for Margate (and even for York and Newcastle, where he had spent only a few adult years) was more like a human relationship than that between a man and a remembered scene. He gives us a hint of this sensibility in *The Best of Life*, when he writes: "Are we not all haunted by certain landscapes that come back unbidden, not as topographical facts but as vestures of the soul? Their charm is within us, and their full meaning incommunicable." Read this in conjunction with another note for which I am indebted to Holbrook Jackson: "I don't think he [Whitten] ever recovered from the translation of Bookseller's Row and Wych Street into Bush House and Aldwych." That is not an exaggeration. Although he was never unsociable, I am sure he found more delight in familiar walks than in the society of other people, and this became more true as increasing deafness hemmed him in.

During the last war he found it necessary to take a staff job again, and he took it, of all places, in the art department of the *Daily Mail*, where he selected photographs and wrote captions. But he hated the routine of a newspaper office, and when in 1919 Grierson invited him to go to Newnes' and start a weekly of his own he jumped at the chance. *T.P.'s* had died three years earlier, and *John o' London's Weekly* quickly established itself, in the easier conditions of peace time, in the vacant place. Its success was largely due, as the success of *T.P.'s* had been due, to a partnership. As Whitten had eighteen years earlier sustained T. P. O'Connor, now his own gifts were very ably reinforced by those of his joint editor, Sidney Dark, and when Dark went elsewhere in 1924, by those of George Blake, who acted as joint editor until 1928. But Whitten's two regular articles, the quaintly named *Letters to Gog and Magog*,*

* A selection of these letters was published in 1926 under the title *Unposted Letters*.

and the *Passing Remarks* signed by "Jackdaw," established the keynote of the paper, and he wrote them almost every week for twenty-three years. His powers had shown no sign of failing, and he seemed to have years of useful service before him, when he fell while taking a walk in the black-out at Margate. He broke a leg, complications set in, and he died three weeks later in Margate General Hospital. In the words of God's promise to Job, he came to his grave "in a full age, like as a shock of corn cometh in in his season."

*   *   *   *   *

To talk with Whitten was always a delight. Although his work might give the impression that he lived in the past he was always a keen newspaper reader, and knew very well what was going on in the world around him. Someone has written of him that he never troubled to keep abreast of contemporary literary movements. That is not quite true. Whenever he came to the office of *John o' London's Weekly*, where I was in constant contact with him from 1928 onwards, he eagerly seized and carried away with him all such publications, for example, as *New Writing* and the work of Ezra Pound and Gertrude Stein, and what he wrote about them is on record. But it is true that he had little sympathy with them, and did not take them very seriously. For modern experimental verse he had no taste at all.

His greatest charm lay in his complete unconsciousness of self. When he was interested in a subject it carried him away completely. He had little small talk, and no lukewarm opinions. If he had nothing to say he said nothing; if he had anything to say he would say it with the utmost vigour, and often at the top of his supple and soaring tenor, wherever he happened to be. My most enduring memory of a Fleet Street wine-bar where I have often sat with him

B

is of a lane of startled faces staring in our direction as Whitten gave me his private opinion on this or that matter in a voice that rattled the glasses on the shelves. It was not aggressiveness that made him do it, and certainly no conscious lack of consideration for others, but simply his complete absorption in what he was saying. On such an occasion I remember his telling me a long and involved story of an experience he had had in a Lyons Corner House. He was entirely unmusical, and the point of the story was that for the first time in his life he thought he recognised a tune the band was playing. He was so moved that he sent a waitress to ask the conductor what it was. The answer came back: "Auld Lang Syne!" He told me this with as much gravity as if a miracle had happened to him.

To Holbrook Jackson, who knew him for more than thirty years, his chubby face and gleaming spectacles "instantly recalled Mr. Pickwick. He not only looked like Mr. Pickwick: he was Pickwickian. He had the same sort of innocence, the same capacity for surprise, the same tendency to get himself entangled in incongruous situations, the same gift of being invincibly himself, and the same unquestioning conservatism of attitude towards life and affairs." He had indeed a tendency to become entangled in incongruous situations. Once, left alone in his house in a northern suburb, he made elaborate preparations for an intensive course of etching, in which art he was at that time engrossed. Turning on the bath-tap, he left his sheets there to soak. Then, noticing that the day was beautifully fine, he suddenly decided to visit St. Albans Cathedral, and etching forgotten, set off there and then. Meanwhile the bath tap went on running, and he returned late that evening to find a steady stream of water flowing under the front door and most of the wallpaper on the ground floor hanging in folds from walls and ceilings. After a period of reflection he decided to do the re-papering himself, and made even more elaborate preparations. Rolls of paper, paste and steps were all placed in position, and his wife and daughter (who tells me the story) heard nothing from him for an hour. Suddenly the silence was broken by strangled cries for help, and Whitten was discovered standing on his steps like a badly wrapped mummy, unable either to see or to move. That was the end of that, but not the end of similar attempts to make himself useful, which usually had the same unfortunate result. He was at once incapable of doing much with his hands, yet always burning to try.

Does all this suggest that he had no sense of humour? Nothing could be further from the truth. No one could have written the essay on Dan Leno, or *The New Canute*, in this book who was unable to see the funny side of life. No one could have kept the light touch in his " Jackdaw" column for so long if a sense of humour had not been an essential part of his make-up. Yet inextricably mixed with it was a childlike innocence that was as genuine as the Mint. It was this, as well as a complete freedom from such baser qualities as envy and uncharitableness, that made him such a lovable colleague and friend. His needs were simple, and if they were provided for he was content. He never over-valued his own powers, and had no ambitions that he could not fulfil. He asked no more of life than to be left alone with his books, to take his daily walks in the country behind Margate—he describes one of them in the essay *Just a Country Walk*—and now and again to meet a few of his cronies in a homely tavern when his day's work was done.

*   *   *   *   *

In making this selection I have been guided by the subjects Whitten most enjoyed writing about. Thus at least eight of the essays are about London, several are about

London worthies, a few illustrate his love of nature, and one or two his concern for the proper use of words.   They are arranged chronologically rather than in groups because this has no claim to be a text-book, but is intended rather as a book to be browsed over at random, and because I thought it interesting to trace the development of Whitten's style. The essays up to and including *Abbeyana*, and the two poems, are from *T.P.'s Weekly*.   The essays from *The Historic Shudder* to the end are from *John o'London's Weekly*. I have made only trifling alterations in the text.   Occasionally statements appear which were true when they were made, but which have been falsified by the passage of time. To have altered some of them would have meant a major operation.   I thought it better to let them stand as a record of the period in which they were written: no one need be misled if he notes the date at the end of each essay.

The attentive reader will doubtless detect the change in Whitten's style as he grew older.   In the early 1900's, when life moved more slowly than it does now, he liked to spread himself.   He was more rhetorical, his beginnings and endings more studied.   See, for example, the last few lines of the first essay, *The Joy of London*, and the first few of *The Soul of the Ready Writer*.   Read also this passage from an early essay, not included in this book, in which he eloquently contrasted the hurly-burly of Blackpool with the glory of the sunsets over the western sea:

The tide goes out and out, until you do not know where the widths of wet sand end or the breathless sea begins.   Great lakes of gold beam up from that desolate floor, on which a few gulls move in remote security. When at last the resplendent sun has broken his fires on the sea-line there remains an immensity of light and trailing vapour that fleers the west with crimson, revealing, maybe, some far-off brighter league, where, in the calm of uttermost distance, the spirit of God moves on the face of the waters.   No man ought to turn from this lit sea to the electric lamps and the Babel of voices without liking them better.   Here is humanity, here is youth, here are love and hope and the chance of happiness, and the girl's laugh which is to be the mother's croon, and that immense recurrence of the human lot which is too plain for youth to see or age to regret.   Near and far the lights move, the white dresses gleam, and the dark falls reluctant on a happy world.

Later on such purple passages become rarer, partly no doubt because of some change in the man himself, partly because literary standards became more austere, but partly too because the nature of his work was different.   In the days of *T.P.'s Weekly* he was a writer-at-large.   In his *John o' London's* days he became primarily a reviewer, and usually a reviewer of new books rather than of new editions of old favourites.   And no one realised better than he, by the way, that unless one is a Macaulay or a Sainte-Beuve the work of those "whose mission is to strike a bliss upon the day" loses much of its virtue with the lapse of time. There are clear hints of self-revelation in *The Soul of the Ready Writer*.   But although he pruned his style with passing years he never lost his faculty for button-holing a reader with his first sentence, and ending with a snap that left him thinking.   The young writer can learn much from a study of his essay-endings.   Let me give a single example, from the essay on Cruden (*How Mad was He?*) on page 157:

On November 1st, 1770, the Corrector, Concordance-maker, Bookseller, Lover and Lunatic failed to appear at breakfast in Camden Street, Islington.   He was found in the powdering closet, his hands clasped, his head upon an open Bible, dead.

Whitten as well as Flaubert knew indeed how to invoke

the historic shudder.   Arnold Bennett, who did not bestow praise lightly, once described him as "one of the finest prose-writers now writing English."

*   *   *   *   *

My acknowledgments are due to Messrs Methuen for kindly permitting me to reproduce the extract from *A Londoner's London*, and to Messrs. George Newnes for the extracts from *John o' London's Weekly*.   I have not been able to establish with certainty who holds the copyright of the extracts from *T.P.'s Weekly*, but I gratefully record that Mr. Holbrook Jackson, Mr. W. J. Ennever and The Amalgamated Press, all of whom had a clear right to be consulted, have courteously waived any claim to it so far as this book is concerned.

THE JOY OF LONDON

WALKING along the Embankment the other day I found a Cockney feeding the gulls from a large brown paper bag filled with sprats. He did it with much solemnity. He did not smile at his gulls, or call them pretty names, or show any emotion whatever. Hundreds of gulls kept flying past him within reach of his hand. Sprat after sprat flew into the air and was instantly caught in a passing beak. Then one gull would fly with extraordinary swiftness out of the mêlée, followed by three or four envious rivals. But the vast majority of these beautiful birds circled back to take their place once more in the endless queue. The effect of the perpetual circling, the punctual sprat, and the grey beauty of the river had in it something hypnotic, and certainly it disposed me to reverie.

It is just such incidents as these—I do not care what they are—that wake into life again a man's appreciation of the beauty, the significance, and the majesty of London. Even on those who love her best, London lays the narcotic spell of her immensity. In the routine and dailyness of life all becomes one colour, one habit; and for days and weeks together the Londoner is apt to sacrifice, without intending it, one of his chief joys—the joy of being where he is.

Until I saw the man with the gulls I do not think it had occurred to me that in bringing these beautiful birds every winter to the Thames, and to the great bridges, Nature has shown herself a fine municipal artist. What could be more fitting than that these wild creatures of the cliff and the wave should wing their way trustfully into the capital of the greatest maritime Power in the world, and establish almost personal relations with its inhabitants? When I have watched the swallows flying over the Louvre in Paris, dipping their wings in the Seine, from which at the same moment urban anglers were drawing silvery fish, I have felt jealous of Paris. To Paris be her swallows. Here again Nature has shown herself a municipal artist. The skimming, fleeting, ever-returning swallows may well feel themselves at home in that city of glitter and change. To London her gulls, for though all rivers run into the sea, none runs thither so surely as the Thames.

The eternal difference between Paris and London, as cities, turns on this difference in their rivers. In Paris the Seine is an incident, whereas it may almost be said that on the Thames London is an incident. At any rate, London itself has not been able—by bridge, wharf, and embankment —to rob the Thames of its character as a great primitive stream which once ran silent under the stars, and bore the howl of wolves down its breezes.

I myself have seen two whales shoot Waterloo Bridge, but I am shy of mentioning the fact because whenever I do so my friends insist that they must have been porpoises! These, however, were whales—a kind of narwhal, I fancy. The thing occurred about fourteen years ago if I remember rightly, and the particulars are necessarily buried in the newspapers of that date. As whales they were small; as visitors to the Thames they were tremendous. I rather enjoy telling the story to Frenchmen. I must also confess to a malicious fondness for that story of the eighteenth century Englishman who, being asked in Paris whether London had a river to compare with the Seine, replied, "Yes, and we call it Fleet Ditch."

Another memory came back when I had seen the last sprat fly over the Embankment parapet. It was the memory of a golden-grey autumn afternoon a good many years ago, and of another little crowd of idlers on the

Embankment. A black object in the water had attracted a languid attention, which developed by degrees into curiosity and grim suspicion as the current brought it, yard by yard, up to the steps near Cleopatra's Needle. I had my own opinion about the nature of that floating object enveloped in black cloth, and on going down the steps to satisfy a restless doubt it proved to be only too correct. I can see now the little boat of the river police putting out from Waterloo Bridge in response to our distant beckoning, and can almost hear the bells of Westminster Abbey ringing gently for afternoon service. Thus beauty and tragedy chase each other through London's daily routine.

The moment one begins to think about London, the more do its associations mingle with all daily happenings. You can live in London without often thinking of its past; yet the past, if you care for it, starts up to greet you everywhere. Two of my friends have just gone to live in Red Lion Square. I wonder if they ever heard of Red Lion Mary? It is good that a servant girl's name should be linked to a Bloomsbury square, and Red Lion Mary seems to have deserved her destiny. She was servant at No. 17, when that house was the home of William Morris, Edward Burne-Jones, and Dante Gabriel Rossetti. She was a plain person, of much character and unfailing good humour —imperturbable, in fact. Rossetti one day bounded into the room, strode up to her, and in tragic tones and with fearful meaning in his voice, exclaimed:

> Shall the hide of a fierce lion
> Be stretched on a couch of wood,
> For a daughter's foot to lie on,
> Stained with a father's blood?

Whereupon the girl, quite unawed by the horrible proposition, replied with complacency: "It shall if you like, sir."

Morris and his friends took No. 17, Red Lion Square, unfurnished, and as I learn from Mrs. E. T. Cook's pleasant *Highways and Byways in London*, it was here that Morris first turned his attention to furniture and decorations. Mrs. Cook does not mention that old Jonas Hanway, the first man to carry an umbrella in London (for which he suffered much contumely), had also decorated a house in Red Lion Square, with the object, as he said, "to relieve the vacuum in social intercourse between the time of assembling and the placing of the card-tables, and to prevent cards from engrossing the whole of my visitors' minds." Why, by the way, has Red Lion Square been deprived of its little dove-cote, which used to be perched on the top of a tall post in its garden? I never go through the square without missing it.

From Red Lion Square there are at least half a dozen egresses, if you know where to find them; and one of them leads, or did lead until yesterday, into Kingsgate Street, where stood the residence of Mrs. Gamp, and where hung the portrait of Mrs. Harris. Who could ever pass the foot of this street, now utterly demolished, without thinking of Mrs. Gamp's panting clients turning the corner in their fateful rush to ply her knocker at some unearthly hour? Until quite recently a Fire Brigade lamp stood at the foot of the street, directing the public to the fire engines, so that to the last Kingsgate Street was a place of scurry and exciting possibilities.

Dickens believed that houses have feelings and recollections, that they cling to life like human beings; yet the destruction of Kingsgate Street is a mere prefatory note to the greatest clearance of London streets that has taken place since the Fire of 1666 ate its way from Pudding Lane to Pie Corner. The streets that are doomed have been stigmatised as slums. Even so, these labyrinthine ways deserve a word of regret. In these tall decrepit houses, on whose red tiles and shaky windows the winter sun sheds a dying gleam, men have been born, men have died, and the bridegroom has brought home his bride.   Even now at night on their narrow asphalt the children dance as though they should never be old; and thus the change and the changelessness of London are seen side by side.   Her present is always pregnant with her future, and in the heart of all her decay and Titanic weariness and plentiful sorrow there is the same abounding energy that, working in other ways, brings the sea gulls to the Embankment.

[*December* 26, 1902.]

HOW I SHOOK HANDS WITH SHAKESPEARE

IT is remarkable how one can overlook one's privileges. Not till the other day did it occur to me that I had shaken hands with Shakespeare.   Indirectly, to be sure. By proxy, of course.   Still, to have shaken hands with Shakespeare at all, to be able to set up the most shadowy claim to such a distinction, is something.   I had been talking to a lady who enjoyed the friendship of John Ruskin, and it was not until she had given me her hand and I had gone my way that the full meaning of this little meeting dawned upon me.

I then remembered an interesting fact in Ruskin's boyhood.   He was taken by a Mr. Pringle to see the aged banker poet, Samuel Rogers, in the big house which to-day, quite unaltered externally, faces the Green Park.   Young Ruskin seems to have borne himself before the venerable poet with considerable assurance; indeed, Mr. Pringle was disappointed in his lack of hero-worship. Ruskin himself tells with quiet humour the story of his rather unsuccessful efforts to ingratiate himself with the author of *The Pleasures of Memory*:

I congratulated him with enthusiasm on the beauty of the engravings by which his poems were illustrated, but betrayed, I fear me, at the same time some lack of an equally vivid interest in the composition of the poems themselves. At all events, Mr. Pringle, I thought at the time, somewhat abruptly diverted the conversation to subjects connected with Africa. These were doubtless more calculated to interest the polished minstrel of St. James' Place; but again I fell into misdemeanours by allowing my own attention, as my wandering eyes too frankly confessed, to determine itself on the pictures glowing from the crimson-silken walls; and accordingly, after we had taken leave, Mr. Pringle took occasion to advise me that, in future, when I was in the company of distinguished men, I should listen more attentively to their conversation.

Thus I shook hands with Samuel Rogers.

Rogers had known Richard Brinsley Sheridan, the author of *The School for Scandal* and of a thousand witticisms, during twenty-five years. He had heard him deliver his great speech in the trial of Warren Hastings; he had foregathered, times without number, with Sheridan, Moore, and Byron; and he was one of the two or three who remained loyal to Sheridan in his last days of debt and dishonour. He had stories to tell of Sheridan's death-bed. Asked by the doctor if he had ever undergone an operation, he answered: "Never, except when sitting for my portrait or having my hair cut." Sheridan was very proud of his eyes, which were magnificent, and he said to Rogers: "Tell Lady Bessborough that my eyes will look up to the coffin lid as brightly as ever."

So I shook hands with Sheridan.

Sheridan had, of course, known Dr. Johnson; indeed, it was Johnson who proposed him as a member of the Literary Club, remarking: "He who has written the two best comedies of his age is surely a considerable man." And Sheridan was duly elected. He had just pleased Johnson greatly by writing a prologue for the tragedy of *Sir Thomas Overbury*, written by his early companion in London, that unhappy poet, Richard Savage. In his prologue Sheridan described very touchingly the wretched life of

> Ill-fated Savage, at whose birth was given
> No present but the Muse, no friend but Heaven.

So I shook hands with Dr. Johnson.

Johnson and ill-fated Savage had starved and struggled as authors together in the streets of London. Johnson once related to Sir Joshua Reynolds how, one night in particular, Savage and he walked round and round St. James' Square for want of a lodging, but in high spirits and full of patriotism denouncing the Government, and swearing they would "stand by their country." When Savage died in want and misery, Johnson anxiously hastened to write his biography, so that the public should receive an authentic and favourable account of his friend. He never wrote anything better than his *Life of Savage*. Of this book Sir Joshua Reynolds said that on his return from Italy he met with it in Devonshire, knowing nothing of its author, and began to read it with his arm against a chimney-piece. It gripped him so strongly that, not being able to lay the book down till he had finished it, he found his arm totally benumbed.

So I shook hands with Richard Savage.

Savage had known Sir Richard Steele, the founder of the *Tatler* and co-worker of Addison on the *Spectator*.

Steele knew Congreve, the brilliant dramatist. He knew him both directly and through Pope. Congreve had a close link with Dryden. It was so close that Dryden hailed Congreve as his successor, and as the guardian of his fame in lines which I cannot resist quoting for their dignity and pathos:

> Already I am worn with cares and age,
> And just abandoning th' ungrateful stage;
> Unprofitably kept at Heaven's expense,
> I live a rent charge on His providence.
> But you, whom every Muse and Grace adorn,
> Whom I foresee to better fortune born,
> Be kind to my remains; and O defend,
> Against your judgment, your departed friend!
> Let not th' insulting foe my fame pursue,
> But shade those laurels which descend to you.

So I shook hands, at a great rate, with Steele, Pope, Congreve and Dryden.

Dryden, you know, once called on Milton at his house in Artillery Walk, near Bunhill Fields, to ask him whether he might turn his *Paradise Lost* into a tragedy in rhyme; and Milton is said to have answered, "Ay, young man, you may tag my verses, if you will"—a surprisingly genial answer to such a request. Whatever the truth of this story may be (one is glad to have Milton into the chain if possible), it is certain that Dryden knew and worked with Sir William Davenant.

I hope I shook hands with Milton, as I did with Davenant.

Davenant was intimate with John Hobbes, the philosopher, who in his youth was secretary to Lord Bacon. He was not, however, Lord Bacon's only famous assistant; Ben Jonson, the great dramatist, was another. So well did Jonson know Bacon that he wrote this account of his talk in his *Discoveries*:—

No man ever spoke more neatly, more pressly, more weightily, or suffered less emptiness, less idleness, in what he uttered. No member of his speech but consisted of his own graces. His hearers could not cough, or look aside from him, without loss. He commanded where he spoke, and had his judges angry and pleased at his devotion. No man had their affections more in his power. The fear of every man that heard him was lest he should make an end.

So I shook hands with the great Hobbes, the greater Bacon, and "Rare Ben."

That Jonson was the friend of Shakespeare, let those doubt who believe that Bacon wrote Shakespeare's plays. Have we not honest Fuller's portrait of them together at the Mermaid?

Many were the wit-combates betwixt Shakespeare and Ben Jonson, which two I behold like a Spanish great galleon and an English man-o'-war. Master Jonson (like the former) was built far higher in learning; solid, but slow in his performances. Shakespeare, with the English man-of-war, lesser in bulk, but lighter in sailing, could turn with all tides, tack about, and take advantage of all winds, by the quickness of his wit and invention.

So I shook hands with Shakespeare. If you look into the matter you will probably find that you have done the same.

[*March* 13, 1903.]

THE PROVERB AND THE TOWN

I HEARD recently of a Hoxton classroom in which not a single boy had ever seen the Thames, with the possible exception of one hopeful, who described it as "what goes past the Tower." This was felt to be deplorable. It may be assumed, however, that many of these lads had been told (with no lack of probability) that they would never set the Thames on fire. London is known to children in the dim ways of legend and proverb long before it is known as an organised reality. A little girl in whose carollings I have the best reason to take delight is continually informing me that "London Bridge is fallen down." "Broken down," you will say; but that is not Sylvia's version, and in a far back number of the *Gentleman's Magazine* I find her justification. "London Bridge is Fallen Down" is there described as an old Christmas carol, belonging specially to Newcastle-on-Tyne. It began:

> Dame, get up and take your pies
> On Christmas Day in the morning.

Other instructions to the dame followed, and she then makes answer or excuse:

> London Bridge is fallen down
> On Christmas Day in the morning.

The inference was that until the Bridge was rebuilt, some stop would be put to the dame's Christmas cooking; but why the falling of London Bridge should form part of a Christmas carol at Newcastle-upon-Tyne I know no more than the ingenious correspondent of the *G. M.* It was in Newcastle that I received my own earliest impressions of London through the medium of song and proverb. A nurse taught me to say:

As I went over London Bridge
I met a cart of hay;
I hit it with my gimmy stick,
And it all flew away.

Perhaps someone else will now tell me what idea she attached to this verse.

A familiar version of the old ballad is this:

London Bridge is broken down;
Dance over the Lady Lea;
London Bridge is broken down,
With a gay Lady [La-dee].

Then we must build it up again.
What shall we build it up withal?
Build it up with iron and steel;
Iron and steel will bend and break.
Build it up with wood and stone;
Wood and stone will fall away.
Build it up with silver and gold;
Silver and gold will be stolen away:
Then we must set a man to watch.
Suppose the man should fall asleep;
Then we must put a pipe in his mouth.
Suppose the pipe should fall and break;
Then we must set a dog to watch.
Suppose the dog should run away;
Then we must chain him to a post.

The two lines in italics are regularly repeated after each line. The Lady Lea, which is to be danced over in apparent derision of the bridgeless Thames, is no other than the River Lea, beloved of anglers for perch and roach. It appears from certain Rolls of Pleas dating from the days of that first Edward, who has just figured so well in the Lord Mayor's Show, that the London Bridge-master had an interest in certain mills on the River Lea near Stratford. But how the connection of ideas in the song arose I do not know, and you may be fairly certain that no one knows.

c

What everyone knows, every "single dweller in the Bills of Mortality," is that "London Bridge is broken down." London has this distinction above all other cities—that its names and symbols have passed into that region of legend and proverb where the critical scoffer lifts his voice in vain.

There are many old sayings about London Bridge which would bear investigation. That which tells us that London Bridge was built upon woolpacks is an obvious reference to the impost on wool which helped to defray its cost. A similar matter-of-fact basis exists for the old saying that London Bridge was made for wise men to go over and fools to go under. This is simply a reference to the danger which for centuries beset the shooting of the bridge by small boats and wherries. The passage of the water was obstructed, not only by the narrowness of the arches, but by corn-mills built in some of the openings, and, later, by water-works. Of the remaining arches some were too narrow, and the few that could be navigated were rendered dangerous by the wild rush of the tide. At floodtide passengers going down the river would disembark at the Old Swan Stairs and walk to Billingsgate, or vice versa. Dr. Johnson and Boswell did this on July 30, 1763, when they hired a sculler at the Temple Stairs for an excursion to Greenwich. Croker, who explains Johnson's procedure in a note, adds: "I had once the honour of attending the Duke and Duchess of York on a party of pleasure down the river, and we were about to land to allow the barge to shoot the bridge. The Duchess asked 'Why?' and being told that it was on account of the danger, positively refused to get out of the boat, and insisted on shooting, which we reluctantly did; but we shipped a good deal of water, and all got very wet, Her Royal Highness showing not the least alarm or regret." Many young Londoners, male and female, were of the same mind as the Duchess. Hence Canning's lines:

"Shoot me the Bridge?"
    The venturous Boatmen cry.
"Shoot me the Bridge!"
    The exulting Fare reply.

The results are:

Drenched each thin garb,
    And clogged each struggling limb,
Far o'er the stream
    The Cocknies sink or swim.

Other proverbs and sayings concerning London Bridge
are numerous, and many of them will be found in Mr. W.
Carew Hazlitt's *English Proverbs and Proverbial Phrases*.
Here are a few:

Like one of the heads on London Bridge, able neither
to speak nor breathe.

It is impossible to stop the tide at London Bridge.

If London Bridge had fewer eyes it would see better.
The last saying refers, of course, to the fewness and
narrowness of the arches.

Perhaps the most familiar of all proverbial sayings about
London is that which warns the unpromising boy that he
will never set the Thames on fire. The demand for some
explanation of a proverb which shall seem erudite has been
responsible for much doubtful lore. I am not enamoured
of the "temse" derivation of this homely and historic
discouragement. We are asked to believe that the old
"temse" or corn-sieve was sometimes set on fire by rapid
manipulation: therefore to tell a lazy fellow that he would
never accomplish the feat was a common reproof. This
may be the origin of the saying, but it is certainly not the
secret of its continuance. To "set the Thames on fire"
is a large and picturesque idea, far above corn-sieves and
dictionaries of phrase and fable. A similar explanation
of the French phrase "to set the Seine on fire" merits the
same comment.

George Augustus Sala doubted whether setting the Thames on fire had much antiquity as an idea, and his note is worth putting on record:

> Unless I am very much mistaken, the antiquaries and the folk-lorists will but waste their time in rummaging among the cobwebs of antiquity for the origin of this phrase. It is to be found in a poem by the second Lord Thurlow (a very simple lord, it would seem) on the Peace of 1814, and dedicated to the Prince Regent. The noble poet goes into raptures over the illuminations and fireworks, some of which were exhibited on the river's bank, and compliments the Regent on having "set the Thames on fire." The absurdly bombastic character of this hyperbole naturally led to his lordship being unmercifully "chaffed" in the critical reviews of the day; and "setting the Thames on fire" became as a locution proverbial. I never read Lord Thurlow's poem in its entirety, but I have a perfect remembrance of seeing it criticised and ridiculed in some "monthly" or "British" review, reference to old volumes of which would doubtless confirm that which I have said. It is possible that as to the year I may be mistaken, but to the presence of the line "Set the Thames on fire" I will swear. The parallel expression in French to "he will never set the Thames on fire" is *not* "he will never set the Seine," but "il n'a pas inventé la poudre," a locution obviously of no great antiquity. Of course, if any reference can be found in last century literature to "setting the Thames on fire" my explanation goes for nothing.

I am not at all certain that the challenge in Sala's last sentence has been met. Mr. Vincent Stuckey Lean, in his vast *Collection*, records the saying without illustrative quotations.

If indolence finds its reproof in the saying I have just

discussed, ambition and industry are fostered in a million nurseries by the saying that London streets are paved with gold. In some versions of the story of Dick Whittington it is related that he was drawn to London by this auriferous report, but whether this is found in the earliest versions I do not know. The saying, however it originated, was vitalised by Henry Carey's ballad, which exclaims:

> O London is a dainty place,
>   A great and gallant city!
> For all the streets are paved with gold,
>   And all the folks are witty.
> And there's your lords and ladies fine,
>   That ride in coach and six;
> That nothing drink but claret wine,
>   And talk of politicks.

The lines "For all the streets are paved with gold, and all the folks are witty" appear to me to be an obscure prophecy of the Limerick craze.

It is around the very oldest of London's fabrics that the largest number of proverbial expressions clusters. St. Paul's, therefore, has its share, and a very pretty old nursery rhyme connects St. Paul's with London Bridge:

> Upon Paul's steeple stands a tree
> As full of apples as may be,
> The little boys of London town
> They run with hooks to pull them down;
> And then they run from hedge to hedge
> Until they come to London Bridge.

"As old as Paul's Steeple" ceased to have any reference to fact in the year 1561 when, in consequence of a severe fire, it was necessary to take the steeple down. "As blunt as Paul's" seems to hint at the first impression made by the Cathedral after the loss of its steeple. A similar fate overtook the analogous saying, "As old as Charing Cross."

The Cross was taken down in 1647.   On the other hand, there was a proverb, derived from Sir Thomas More, which said: "Paul's will not always stand."   There is a premonition of London's end, also, in the saying "Canterbury was, London is, and York shall be."

A very curious old toast, which is possibly given now and then, even to-day, is "All friends round St. Paul's, not forgetting the Tree, and the Trunkmaker's Daughter." A contributor to "Notes and Queries" in 1871 describes a dinner of commercial travellers at which this toast was solemnly given.   I think it not improbable that it was a favourite with commercial travellers hailing from London. The toast dates from the eighteenth century, and according to an explanation printed in the *Leisure Hour* and adopted by Mr. Hazlitt, the actual trunkmaker referred to had his shop at No. 74, St. Paul's Churchyard.   It was his pretty daughter who was long commemorated in the toast.   Mr. Henry Nickless, the trunkmaker in question, died on November 18, 1750, and was described in an obituary notice as "Master of the famous trunk maker's shop at the corner of St. Paul's Churchyard, worth twenty thousand pounds."   He figures in Hogarth's print of "Beer." "The trunk maker" was a phrase common in the last and present century (it is once or twice alluded to in Macaulay's Essays) as the bourne to which unsaleable books were commonly consigned as waste-paper by their unfortunate publishers.   Lord Byron, in his *Ravenna Journal*, notes with caustic humour: "After all, it is but passing from one counter to another, from the booksellers to the other tradesmen, grocer or pastrycook.   For my part, I have met with some poetry upon trunks, so that I am apt to consider the trunk maker as the sexton of authorship."

Few things are older than Newgate, and few excite the popular imagination more than the death penalty.   There is, therefore, a series of sayings about the most famous of prisons. Many of them connect it, by what was once the most easy of associations, with Tyburn. "He that is at a low ebb at Newgate may soon be afloat at Tyburn," was the ironical description of the condemned prisoner. A very curious saying was "He will faint at the sight of a wallflower," applied to persons who had reasons to dread the administrations of the turnkey or hangman. It appears to have originated in the simple fact that wallflowers once grew up the side of Newgate. "He will ride backwards up Holborn Hill" referred to the last journey of a criminal from Newgate to Tyburn. There were all kinds of humorous periphrases for the last act of the law. An execution was called "Paddington Fair." The hangman's noose was known variously as a "Tyburn tippet," or a "Paddington pair of spectacles." To be hanged was to "preach at Tyburn Cross." As the sermons were short, it was said:

> Suits hang half a year in Westminster Hall,
> At Tyburn half an hour's hanging endeth all.

On the whole, the best comfort offered to malefactors was that which conveyed the hope of mercy in the saying, "A London jury hang half and save half."

But the proverbial philosophy of London is not confined to a few of its greatest features. Scores of its streets and institutions have inspired that wit of one which is the wisdom of many. Do people talk now of "going on a pig to Putney"? For some reason, lost in the backward files of time, if a person said he was going to Putney it was considered amusing to answer: "What! on a pig?" Mr. Hazlitt has heard that the old boys that plied up the river carried signs at the bow, and that one of these—perhaps the best remembered—was a pig. "Go to Putney!" was sometimes heard in the same sense as "Go to Jericho!" or, as in Newcastle-on-Tyne, "Go to Hexham!" There was a sad wisdom in the proverb: "Love and pride stock Bedlam." "Covent Garden is the best garden" voiced the experience that raising flowers and vegetables oneself is not so cheap as coming to the London market. It was also said: "Cheapside is the best garden." "As melancholy as Fleet Street in the long vacation" explains itself, and is less exaggerated than "In October not even a cat is to be found in London." I forget who it was who corrected both these sayings in the remark that "London is the best place in England to live in for eight months of the year, and as good as any other for the rest."

The poverty of budding lawyers is grimly touched off in the saying: "The gentlemen of Furnival's Inn lie abed while their hose are mending." "All Lombard Street to a China orange" was the equivalent of "A thousand pounds to a penny." Sometimes it was "All Lombard Street to an eggshell." "He must take him a house in Turnagain Lane" was said of a man who had embarked on some course of action from which it seemed certain he would have to retreat. Scottish valour in battle seems to be indicated in the saying: "As tattered as the Scots colours in Westminster Hall."

Perhaps the popular prejudice against lawyers never found more withering expression than in the saying: "The Devil would have been a weaver, but for the Temples." Another side of this feeling is reflected in the saying: "I'll make him water his horse at Highgate," used, no doubt, less in London than in country towns north of the metropolis. It was equivalent to a threat of legal proceedings, and meant, "I will compel him to take a journey to London to defend himself." It was in the provinces, and, according to Mr. Stuckey Lean, in Cheshire, that London affectations were hit off in the saying: "She hath been at London to call a strea a straw and waw a wall." "They agree like London clocks" was not complimentary to a man and his wife. Space forbids me to mention or discuss many other alliances between the Proverb and the Town. I conclude, therefore, by abruptly wishing my readers a Happy Christmas, in which they shall be able to say, with my last proverb, "I have dined as well as my Lord Mayor of London."

[*Undated: about* 1904.]

AT THE SIGN OF THE PILLOW

LORD ROSEBERY recently advised people who suffer from insomnia to read Cockburn's letters to his gardener; he said they belonged to "that rare collection of books which people could enjoy by their bedside, not as literary opiates, but because they were pleasant and healthy to read, which they could break off at any minute when they felt drowsy, and which left a pleasant impression on them when they laid them down." Immediately there was uproar. The doctors proclaimed that no books are "healthy to read" in bed. They recited, with medical variations, the words of Biron in *Love's Labour's Lost*:

> Why, all delights are vain; but that most vain,
> Which with pain purchased doth inherit pain,
> As, painfully to pore upon a book;
>   .   .   .   .   .
> So, ere you find where light in darkness lies
> Your light grows dark by losing of your eyes.

The minds of bed-readers were disturbed. Thereupon scores of experts, gospellers, and brother's keepers came to them with confirmatory warnings of consolatory pooh-ings. To such a pitch of solemnity has the controversy (non-extant two months ago) risen, that a librarian, "who has studied the subject from a practical point of view" has laid down the essentials of the "ideal bedbook." They are alleged to be:

Paper: Pure white with rough surface.
Type: Small Pica Roman.
Weight: 12 oz. to 16 oz.
Depth: $6\frac{1}{2}$ inches.
Width: 5 inches.
Margin at top: $\frac{3}{4}$ inch.
Margin at each side: $1\frac{1}{4}$ inches.
Margin at bottom: $1\frac{3}{4}$ inches.

Quantity of letterpress: 4 inches deep, $2\frac{3}{4}$ inches wide. All of which—in Carlyle's speech—"I, for the present, content myself with modestly but peremptorily and irrevocably denying." Not because I think it is wrong, but because I think it is "impidence." Life is simpler than that.

The ideal bed-book is the sort of bed-book you like best, taken from your own shelves. It is not necessary to have a book specially made up for you from a librarian's prescription, though I confidently expect a Bed-Book Series to be announced shortly, with a Harley Street testimonial on each fly-leaf. I have certainly no theories of my own to offer. My preference, now I come to think of it, is for the lightest of mental as of bodily suppers. Reading a good novel in bed is delightful; but if it grips you it is an injustice to your sleep; and if sleeps prevails, as it must, it is an injustice to the novel. Commend me to brevities of thought or anecdote, so that at any moment I may say: This is good, on this I will rest. For I like to fall asleep definitely laughing, or definitely inspired; I refuse "to be continued" in one mood or the other. Sufficient unto the night is the good thing thereof. Last night, as it happened, I reposed on this story of an Indian judge, told by the Right Hon. Sir Mountstuart E. Grant Duff in his *Notes from a Diary*:

It was in the district immediately to the north—in Ganjam—that the judge lived whose method of deciding cases was beautifully simple. He used, when the time to give his judgment came, to count the flies on the punkah. If the number was even he gave it for the plaintiff; if odd, for the defendant. The name of this worthy is habitually cited when the anecdote is told in this Presidency.

An admirable judge: waking, he did not worry, why should you—sleeping?

Of course, I do not limit myself to one morsel. But I infallibly recognise the one on which to extinguish my lamp. One story is too moving, another too bitter, another is too provocative of thought. This, for instance, is too moving:

Mrs Godfrey Clerk mentioned at dinner to-day that during the battle of Meeanee Sir John Pennefather, who had been waiting by his horse till the order came for him to go into action, suddenly received it. He mounted, and turning to his troopers, said "God forgive me, my boys, for having told your mothers I'd take care o' ye!"

An old examination story flashed pleasantly on the eye as the pages turned:

"Explain Lupercalia." Answer: "Lupercalia was the she-wolf that nursed Romeo and Juliet!"

I like this foraging among old and new, grave and gay, poetic and flippant; it is an epitome of the mixed world from which one is about to retire into the half world of dreams. Let what will flash and beckon in the turning of the pages —as the land quaintly twists and assembles itself to the eye when you view it from a departing ship. Questions that you cannot stay to argue, opinions that you need not controvert, curious dicta. As thus:

A lady mentioned, at dinner, that Swinburne had

asked her what were the two finest lines in the language. He answered his own question by quoting from *Sordello*:

> As the king-bird, with ages on his plumes
> Travels to die in his ancestral glooms.

A fine picture and a haunting. But the "two finest lines in the language"? That is debatable, though not to be debated. These personal preferences are most interesting, though in Mr. Swinburne's case, the isolation of these lines is qualified by the well-known fact that Mr Swinburne's generous and fervent appreciation of the last fine piece of literature he has read is wont to express itself in a blaze of superlatives. A well known poet of to-day once told me that he knew of no finer lines in the language than Iago's soliloquy as he sees Othello about to fall into his infamous trap—a villain's compassion for his victim:

> Not poppy nor mandragora
> Nor all the drowsy syrups of the world
> Shall ever medicine thee to that sweet sleep
> Which thou owedst yesterday.

Who does not enjoy these little gifts of literature from a hand skilled to cull?

A verse that reminds you of another verse, a story that recalls another story, these are companionable things, and the book that contains them is my "ideal bed-book." Another page gave me last night:

> Mr. Glennie, with whom I rode and walked to-day, told me that he once heard a gentleman say at dinner, "I did not know that such and such was a taxidermist." "A taxidermist!" broke in another guest, "Why he's a European."

Which reminds me of a better and (to me) a nearer story. A journalistic friend of mine, who was "doing" Henley Regatta, ignored a trespass board, and was half-way across some fields toward the river when a rural policeman stopped him saying: "Didn't you see that there notice: 'This Path is Closed to Pedestrians'?" "But," retorted my friend, "I am not a pedestrian, I am a Congregationalist," and was allowed to pass by the nonplussed officer. Here, again, is an ideal bit of pillow philosophy. Sir Grant Duff says that George Boyle quoted it to him as a translation, or a paraphrase, of some lines of Goethe's, and that he has often drawn comfort from it in public and in private life:

> But on the ice-covered heights of Armenia,
> And in the dark forests of far Abyssinia,
> Still spake the oracle, just as before.
> Child of the world, leave fools to their foolishness!
> Things to their natures, and mules to their mulishness,
> Berries were bitter in forests of yore!

[March 4, 1904.]

THE MUFFIN MAN

> Vague Genius of the square and street!
> Who marks his coming or retreat?
> Anon some area-tripping maid
> Involves him in a moment's trade,
> Some housewife drops, with simper bland,
> A cautious twopence in his hand. . . .
> His bell! Again, again, again,
> It steals upon an idle brain,
> Till life, enchanted, seems to swoon
> To one long London afternoon.
> Faint pulse of Time in London's ear,
> Yet type of all her Now and Here,
> Survivor still of every knell,
> How wisely drones the Muffin Bell!
> Lo he, who eyes each door askance,
> Is sealed a priest of Circumstance.

[February 13, 1903.]

RAINY DAY SMITH

A CORRESPONDENT asks me where he can obtain a work which I have frequently mentioned—John Thomas Smith's *Book for a Rainy Day: or, Recollections of the Events of the Last Sixty Years* (1766–1833). It has long been out of print, and is therefore to be found only in the second-hand bookshops, where a copy never remains unsold. In this and all such cases the best plan is to ask the bookseller to procure the volume, naming the highest price you are willing to pay for it. The *Rainy Day* is not a big book, but its three hundred octavo pages are as full of interest as an egg is of meat. The first edition appeared in 1845, twelve years after Smith's death, and a second edition appeared in the same year. This I have rarely met with, but the third edition of 1861 is fairly common, and can sometimes be bought for three or four shillings.

John Thomas Smith was a veritable Londoner. He was born in a London hackney coach on the evening of the 23rd of June, 1766. His mother had spent the evening at the house of her brother, Mr. Edward Tarr, a "convivial glass-grinder," of Earl Street, Seven Dials, and the coach was conveying her back with necessary haste to her home at No. 7, Great Portland Street. Sixty-seven years later the man who had entered thus hurriedly into the world left it with almost equal unexpectedness in his house, No. 22, University Street, after holding for seventeen years the post of Keeper of the Prints at the British Museum. Smith's life covers thirty-three years of the eighteenth century and thirty-three of the nineteenth, a period which for readers of to-day lends a centenary interest to his accounts of London.

Almost as soon as Mrs. Smith's hackney coach had brought her to No. 7, Great Portland Street—a house whose site is now covered, as I reckon, by No. 38—Dr. William Hunter, brother of the great John Hunter, arrived from Jermyn Street, and performed his duties with the skill of a Physician-Extraordinary to the Queen. The attendance of such a man proves the material comfort of the Smith family. Nathaniel Smith, the flustered father, was principal assistant to Joseph Nollekens, the sculptor, and he had worked for Joseph Wilton and the great Roubiliac. For Wilton he carved three of the nine masks representing Ocean and eight British rivers—now seen on the Strand front of Somerset House. Smith's mother had been a Miss Tarr, a Quakeress; she died in 1779, when her son was thirteen years of age. Their boy's christening was dictated by family history. He was named John after his grandfather, a Shropshire clothier, whose bust, modelled by Nathaniel Smith, was the first publicly exhibited by the Associated Artists at Spring Gardens; and Thomas after his great uncle, Admiral Thomas Smith, who had earned in Portsmouth Harbour (more cheaply, perhaps, than Smith would have allowed) the name of "Tom of Ten Thousand."

Very early in life Smith went into training to be a gossiping topographer. Old Nollekens, already a Royal Academician and the most sought-after sculptor of portrait busts ("Well, sir, I think my friend Joe Nollekens can chop out a head with any of them" was Johnson's tribute), often took his assistant's little son for a ramble round the streets, pointing out buildings and other details, and recalling interesting characters he had known. One day, coming from his frowsy studio in Mortimer Street, he led Thomas to the Oxford Road to see Jack Rann go by on the cart to Tyburn, where he was to be hanged for robbing Dr William Bell of his watch and eighteen-pence. The boy remembered all his life the criminal's pea-green coat, his nankin small clothes, and the immense nosegay that had been presented to him at St. Sepulchre's steps. In another walk Mr. Nollekens showed him the ruins of the Duke of Monmouth's house in Soho Square. In a Sunday morning ramble they watched the boys bathing in Marylebone Basin, on the site of Portland Place. Or they stood at the top of Rathbone Place while Nollekens recalled the mill from which Windmill Street was named, and the halfpenny hatch which had admitted people to the miller's grounds.

In the studio of Nollekens in Mortimer Street young Smith was useful to his father and to the great bust sculptor. Here he saw many notable people. One day Charles Townley, the collector of the Townley Marbles, noticed him, and "pouched" him half a guinea to purchase paper and chalk. Dr. Johnson, who was sitting for his bust, one day looked at the boy's drawing, and, laying his hand heavily on his head, remarked: "Very well; very well." Later, he entered the studio of John K. Sherwin, the engraver. Here he received a kiss from the beautiful "Perdita," and when Mrs. Siddons sat to Sherwin for her portrait as the Grecian Daughter he raised and lowered the window curtains to obtain the effect of light. Sherwin, unfortunately, was an irregular young man, and his fortunes were declining. Some three years passed, and Smith launched out as a young drawing-master, pencil-portrait draughtsman, and topographical engraver. Sir Joshua Reynolds engaged him to bid for him at auctions. He was a frequent visitor to the drawing-room of Mrs. Mathew, in Rathbone Place, where Flaxman was often found, and where he heard William Blake read his early poems.

Of Smith's reign in the Print Room of the British Museum (1816–1833) not much is known. Then, as now, the British Museum was a world to itself, but the Print Department was not nearly so large or important as it is to-day. The public room is now a temple of art, but in Smith's time it seems to have been a den of anecdotists. One day it is Nollekens, accompanied by Mr. Gibson and Mr. Bonomi, the sculptors, who has come to see him soon after his appointment. They all walk round the Elgin Room, the old sculptor muttering and exclaiming in the petulance of age: "There, you see—look at that shoulder and a part of the breast—look at the veins! The ancients *did* put veins to their gods, though my old friend, Gavin Hamilton, would have it they never did." Button-holeing Smith as they descend to the Townley Gallery, he says: "Now you stand where Queen Charlotte *sat* when she came to the Museum; they brought her a chair, and I stood on the steps below." On another day Mrs. Garrick calls by appointment to see the collection of her dead husband's portraits.

Had John Thomas Smith been granted the scriptural span of life, and a little more, he would have seen the dawn of the Victorian era. Had he lived only three years longer he might have read the *Pickwick Papers*. As it was, he had seen and heard much that was interesting. In a friend's biographical album (he was great on albums and all such means of *getting to know*) John Thomas Smith wrote:

I can boast of seven events, some of which great men would be proud of.

I received a kiss when a boy from the beautiful Mrs. Robinson;

Was patted on the head by Dr. Johnson;

Have frequently held Sir Joshua Reynolds's spectacles;

Partook of a pint of porter with an elephant;

Saved Lady Hamilton from falling when the melancholy news arrived of Lord Nelson's death (Smith tells this story somewhat differently in the *Rainy Day*);

Three times conversed with King George the Third;

And was shut up in a room with Mr. Kean's lion.

But the implacable call came in March, 1833, and he left his life's work unfinished. When he was laid to his rest in St. George's Burial Ground, in the Bayswater

D

Road, he was not yet known as "Rainy Day" Smith. It was, as I have said, twelve years later, in 1845, that the book from which he has this name was published. It has always been esteemed a sociable book—a book full of crannies and corners, a museum, portrait-gallery, and lumber-room book, a book for a rainy day.

[*May* 27, 1904.]

A PAGE FROM THE NEWGATE CALENDAR

IF one thing interests me more than the history of London it is the history of Londoners. By Londoners I mean the nameless millions who walked these streets before us, with all their forgotten business and desires. Here and there some historical chance or odd association has preserved the record of an obscure life. The writings of Defoe are as rich in them as any I know, and in odd corners of print you may have these unlikely glimpses. In one place, to be sure, the very limelight is thrown on the insignificant past, and that is in the records of crime. Therefore I like to read the Newgate Calendar—sometimes. A story I read last night in that amazing register interested me by its mere commonplaceness and obscurity, by the fact, too, that it concerns an erring citizen, and not a mere criminal. Away back in the eighteenth century—to be precise, in 1770—the thing happened, was talked about, and forgotten. I will tell it you, this far-off newspaper story of the Bishopsgate tradesman who was hanged at Tyburn.

John Stretton was well brought up, and in his youth

was apprenticed to the grocery business. He served his time faithfully, winning the good graces of his master and of all who knew him. The paths of grocery opened fair before John Stretton. The next thing was to become a journeyman, and the young man was soon installed in that position with a grocer in Bishopsgate Street. He kept the situation for several years, during which he married and was blessed with a daughter. Then his wife died, and Stretton, still full of energy, determined to be a grocer on his own account. With his savings he set up for himself in Bishopsgate Street, and being known as a safe and regular man he could obtain whatever reasonable credit he desired. He now thought to advance himself still further by a second, and a prudent, marriage.

Mr. John Dabbs, a Bishopsgate butcher, had a daughter, and to her John Stretton began to pay his addresses. He looked for money, but there is no reason to suppose that he did not love Mary Dabbs. Indeed, the girl and her mother were soon warmly on his side, and it was only the purse-sensitive father who blocked the way. Mr. Dabbs had no desire to give his daughter a dowry which would be transferred to the pocket of a young tradesman whose position he perhaps regarded with some little contempt. However, the lovers met frequently, and Mary Dabbs kept Stretton duly informed of her father's tantrums and obstinacy. These accounts caused him much trouble, and a severe illness into which he fell gave him the more time in which to ponder the situation. While confined to his bed he was often visited by the girl and her mother. But unfortunately the quiet of the sick-room brought no calm thoughts to this ambitious grocer. In the starchy diction of the Newgate Calendar, "Chagrined by the father's determination, and resolved to move the objection which seemed to arise from his presumed poverty, he made the dreadful resolution of robbing the mail."

He selected the North mail.   With its coming and going he would be familiar, the General Post Office being then situated in Lombard Street.   Stretton went about his enterprise with a tradesman's timidity, and, indeed, his design was less daring than it sounds.   In 1770 His Majesty's mail was neither a punctual nor an imposing institution.   Fourteen years were to elapse before Mr. John Palmer, of Bath, should introduce regular mail coaches with armed attendants.   In 1770, when the annual revenue of the Post Office was probably not more than £120,000, a robber had to reckon only with a pack-horse or a light cart.   Such robberies were a frequent and obvious way of filling a desperate pocket.   Still, grocers did not often leave their snug shops to rob the mail at two o'clock in the morning.   Stretton knew that at this hour the mail from the North of England would be on its way down the City Road into London.   This road, which had been made only nine years before, ran between fields and market gardens.   Even now the City Road has a wide highway aspect, and is a road between places rather than a domesticated London street.   After its rural beginning, it set out to be genteel and residential, but for many years it has been a medley of broken purposes and new resolves. Chiefly as a roaring tram route does the City Road now fulfil itself, but on a summer morning in 1770 it would be lonesome enough.

On a Saturday night in June, when honest grocery had given him its last halfpenny for the week, John Stretton turned highwayman.   It was a little after midnight when, his shopman being asleep, he stole away from the comfortable odour of his teas and spices to the City Road.   Just behind the present site of St. Luke's Hospital was a famous little resort called "Peerless Pool," an open-air pond fitted as a large pleasure-bath.   Originally called Perilous Pool from its depth, it had been made safe and profitable by a

Mr. William Kemp, who added a fish pond. Peerless Street still marks the site of these places. Near this spot John Stretton, grocer and ratepayer, waited for the mail. He heard it far off, clinking down the long silent road from Islington; heard the increasing sound stop, it may be, at the turnpike which then barred the road half-way down the hill from the Angel; and a little later could tell when it was passing the Shepherd and Shepherdess. In two minutes it would be round the bend. He had these two minutes, and a minute more, in which to snatch salvation out of madness. But he was hypnotised by his design, and virtue and grocery were far away. The post-boy came cheerily on. John Stretton stopped him and terrorised him. He then rifled the letter bags, and, seizing such of these as he fancied, made off into the dark and deserted Moorfields. Here he stuffed his pockets with whatever notes and drafts he could find. Mary Dabbs slept in her home half a mile away.

John Stretton felt that he could now impress the too prudent butcher. He renewed his attentions to his daughter, and his wrangles about money with Mr. Dabbs. The Postmaster-General had offered the usual reward of £200 for the apprehension of the robber, but weeks went by and no one suspected a Bishopsgate tea dealer. Stretton's detection was his own work. He had succeeded, against all probability, as a trembling highwayman; and now he undid himself, against all probability, as a rash man of business. One day, in his anxiety to secure Mr. Dabbs as his father-in-law, he showed him some drafts in his possession, and then, to prove that they were good, he had the incredible folly to summon a porter and send him to cash the drafts at the bank of Boldero, Kendall, and Adey, which, like the Post Office, was in long-suffering Lombard Street. The man, on showing the papers at the bank, was at once challenged, and an officer returned with

him to make inquiries.   Stretton was found behind his
counter.   Asked how he came to possess a certain note,
he replied that he had taken it in the course of business
from a man in Bond Street.   He was taken there in a coach
and invited to find this person; when, on his failing to do
so, he was arrested and brought before that astute blind
man and justice of the peace, Sir John Fielding, half-
brother of the author of *Tom Jones*.   The other missing
notes were found at Stretton's house, and on this evidence
he was judged to have been himself the robber.   Yet he
continually protested his innocence, and even on the
morning of his execution, when he was brought down
into the press-yard to have his irons knocked off, he still
denied the crime, though he was otherwise subdued and
penitent.   An immense crowd, rendered curious by his
persistency, followed the fatal cart to Tyburn.   History
is silent on the butcher's comments and his daughter's
tears, and if I have revived what seems a sordid tale, it is
because into it one can read much human interest and
historical suggestion.

[*June* 10, 1904.]

DR. JOHNSON: THE TALKER*

THE chief ingredients of Dr. Johnson's talk may
safely be set down as wit, common sense, and information.   For that matter these are the ingredients of nearly
all good talk, but Johnson had them in overwhelming
abundance.   I do not know that they were ever more
clearly exhibited, or more shrewdly perceived, than in

* *The Life of Samuel Johnson*, by James Boswell.   Edited, with Notes
and a Biographical Dictionary of the Persons named in the Work, by Percy
Fitzgerald, M.A., F.S.A. (Bliss, Sands, 3*s*. 6*d*.).

Scotland. It was just possible that Johnson might have suffered a diminution of his glory there. Removed from the atmosphere of Fleet Street, deprived of his regular fuglemen and admirers, he might have failed to make that impression on the hard-headed and intensely observant Scots that was in Boswell's hopes. But no such catastrophe occurred. "*He is a dungeon of wit*," said Lady Lochbuy in the desolation of Moy. "*This man is just a hogshead of sense*," exclaimed Mr. Alexander McLean, the worthy doctor in Mull. "*It is music to hear this man speak*," was the verdict of Ulinish when Johnson had explained —the entire process of tanning!

I

Yet wit however bright, sense however strong, and information however extensive, will not necessarily command a submissive hearing. All comes back to the man who wields these weapons. Johnson's form was huge, and his voice majestic. When he talked he was like a mountain in parturition, and it has been suggested that sometimes the mountain brought forth a mouse. "Dr. Johnson's sayings would not appear so extraordinary were it not for his *bow-wow* way," was the remark of Lord Pembroke. Very recently the same thing was said to me in other words by a most intelligent young friend, who this summer took Boswell for his holiday-reading. Bringing to the book a fresh uncoloured view, and a sturdy initiative of mind that had been practised and hardened in the Boer War, this young reader met me on his return with no exclamations of hero-worship. He considered that Johnson's wisdom was exaggerated, and that much of his talk would in anyone else's mouth be considered only ordinary good sense. He complained, also, with a soldier's instinct, that Johnson did not fight his conversational battles to a finish; that when driven into a corner he took refuge in rudeness or in some more or less brutal evasion. I was glad to hear all this. "You will be a Johnsonian," I ventured to predict. For, at least, he had begun with a mind, and mind was the soul of Johnson's conversation. He disliked subservient agreement and a too flattering response. To a man who laughed too readily at his wit he turned and said: "Sir, have I said anything that you understand? Then I ask pardon of the rest of the company."

II

The intrinsic rightness of the opinions expressed by Dr. Johnson in conversation has little to do with his powers as a talker. If he had not been often and impressively in the right he could not have become the literary dictator of his age. He talked for victory. He did not discourse lonesomely and at large, like Coleridge. He talked because he was talked to, and his aim was to set right what he thought had been said amiss: one foe crushed, one fallacy exposed, he was ready for the next. "May there not," pleaded Boswell with him one day, "may there not, Sir, be very good conversation without a contest for superiority?" Johnson replied: "No *animated* conversation, Sir." Nothing but animated talk served him. He liked a man who "fairly sets his mind to yours." Every conversation was a battlefield, and the reek and tumble of it haunted the room next morning. Boswell once found him highly satisfied with his prowess on the preceding evening. "Well, we had a good talk." "Yes, Sir," said Boswell, "you tossed and gored several persons." When we read, therefore, we are not to consider whether Johnson was always just or right. He was often neither, and knew it. He simply refused to be beaten, and when he could no longer rely on reason he fell back on his personality, even on violence. But few whom he crushed bore him malice;

they were only too glad to be tossed and gored again if they might sit under the spell of the Great Cham of literature. It was not as though the same violence was exhibited on the same topics. The infinite variety of Johnson's knowledge and experience filled his hearers with curiosity; there was always the sporting chance of seeing him nonplussed: was there no end to him? His listeners never saw it, and Johnson seems to have been conscious that he was impregnable.

Goldsmith once suggested that some new member should be brought into the Literary Club to give it variety, for, he said: "There can now be nothing new among us; we have travelled over one another's minds." "Sir," said Johnson, "you have not travelled over *my* mind, I promise you." The great mind of Burke never failed to do homage to his friend's herculean powers. Once when he and Stephen Langton were walking home Burke remarked that Johnson had been very great that night. Langton agreed, but said he wished to have heard more from another person (plainly indicating Burke himself). "O no," said Burke, "it is enough for me to have rung the bell to him."

III

Let me illustrate the distinction I draw between the intrinsic value of Dr. Johnson's talk and its fighting value. Not that he is in a very fighting mood in the following passage; but one may usefully note that while Johnson's opinions on gardening might fare badly at the hands of an expert, yet the vigour and insight of his talk on this subject are the utmost that could be expected from a literary man and a town-dweller. He and Boswell were sitting on the stone seats of his garden door in Bolt Court: he was in a placid frame of mind:

Boswell: I wish to have a good walled garden.

Johnson: I don't think it would be worth the expense to you. We compute in England a park-wall at a thousand pounds a mile; now a garden-wall must cost at least as much. You intend your trees should grow higher than a deer will leap. Now let us see—for a hundred pounds you could only have forty-four square yards, which is very little; for two hundred pounds you may have eighty-four square yards, which is very well. But when will you get the value of two hundred pounds of walls, in fruit, in your climate? No, sir, such contention with Nature is not worth while. I would plant an orchard, and have plenty of such fruit as ripens well in your country. My friend, Dr. Madden, of Ireland, said that "in an orchard there should be enough to eat, enough to lay up, enough to be stolen, and enough to rot upon the ground." Cherries are an early fruit; you may have them, and you may have the early apples and pears.

Boswell: We cannot have nonpareils.

Johnson: Sir, you can no more have nonpareils than you can have grapes.

Boswell: We have them, Sir; but they are very bad.

Johnson: Nay, Sir, never try to have a thing merely to show that you *cannot* have it. From ground that would let for forty shillings you may have a large orchard; and you see it costs you only forty shillings. Nay, you may graze the ground when the trees are grown up; you cannot while they are young.

Boswell: Is not a good garden a very common thing in England, Sir?

Johnson: Not so common, Sir, as you imagine. In Lincolnshire there is hardly an orchard; in Staffordshire very little fruit.

Boswell: Has Langton no orchard?

Johnson: No, Sir.

Boswell: How so, Sir?

Johnson: Why, Sir, from the general negligence of the country. He has it not, because nobody else has it.

Boswell: A hot-house is a certain thing; I may have that.

Johnson: A hot-house is pretty certain; but you must first build it, then you must keep fires in it, and you must have a gardener to take care of it.

Boswell: But if I have a gardener, at any rate——

Johnson: Why, yes.

Boswell: I'd have it near my house; there is no need to have it in the orchard.

Johnson: Yes, I'd have it near my house. I would plant a great many currants; the fruit is good, and they make a pretty sweetmeat.

In the same conversation Johnson explains exactly how the pickers-up of bones in the London streets turn their hoards to account. At Corrichatachin, Hebrides, Johnson talked about threshing. An expert might have said this or that; but consider what is available in a literary company, and then consider the pith and insight of Johnson's observations on the difficulty of bargaining with a thresher:

If you pay him by the day's wages he will thresh no more than he pleases; though, to be sure, the negligence of a thresher is more easily detected than that of most labourers, because he must always make a sound while he works. If you pay him by the piece—by the quantity of grain which he produces—he will thresh only while the grain comes freely, and though he leaves a good deal in the ear it is not worth while to thresh the straw over again; nor can you fix him to do it sufficiently, because it is so difficult to prove how much less a man threshes than he ought to do. Here, then, is a dilemma; but, for my part, I would rather trust his idleness than his fraud.

The *form* of this little discourse is worth studying. It

is good without passing out of the colloquial. Johnson admitted that he had made it his constant rule to talk as well as he could both as to sentiment and expression; the consequence, as Sir Joshua Reynolds observed, was that "his common conversation in all companies was such as to secure him universal attention, as something above the usual colloquial style was expected." Did Johnson air his knowledge on out-of-the-way subjects through vanity? Very seldom, one thinks, for opportunities to distinguish himself rose so frequently in a natural way. He could meet any topic. Once when he had expounded the making of gunpowder he confessed to Boswell that he had "talked ostentatiously."

IV

Facts, however, are only the dead bricks of conversation. Mr. Augustine Birrell points out that a good deal of what is called table-talk is only extracts from commonplace books. To be a great table-talker "you must have first a marked and constant character, and, second, the gift of characteristic expression, so as to stamp all your utterances, however varied, however flatly contradictory one with another, with certain recognisable ever present marks or notes." This is precisely Johnson's strength. And this constancy of character in his talk goes far deeper than his mannerisms, his "Yes, sir," and "No, sir," and "Why not, sir?" He had discovered a way of unburdening his mind on all subjects that was definitely his own. Mr. Birrell refers to John Thomas Smith's story of seeing Johnson grapple with a sturdy thief in Grosvenor Square, and his encounter with a Thames bargee; the qualities apparent in these acts, he points out, went into his talk and made it what it is. "It is the old story; anybody can write like Shakespeare if he has the mind." The man who talked with Johnson was wise if he expected contradiction or chastisement; he was pretty sure to get both. But the Doctor's was not often the violence of mere temper, it was the violence of conviction. In some cases, indeed, it seems a noble thing that a man should be so angry as Johnson was on matters which would not ruffle most natures. His detestation of Hume's infidelity led him into a most grotesque encounter with Adam Smith, who had written a high tribute to Hume's character. They met in Glasgow. Smith, fresh from the interview, was asked what had passed. At first he would only reply. "He's a brute—he's a brute"; but afterwards explained that Johnson had attacked him violently about his praise of Hume. "What did Johnson say?" was the eager question put from all sides. "Why, he said," answered Smith, "he said, ' *You lie!* '" To this Smith had made an answer that is merely unprintable. "On such terms," says Sir Walter Scott, who tells the story, did these two great moralists meet, and such was the classical dialogue between these two great teachers of philosophy." This was at least the violence of conviction (on both sides).

V

It must be admitted that the Doctor often exhibited the violence of prejudice. "I am willing to love all mankind except an American," he once roared, and called Americans by every hard name he could muster. Miss Seward, looking at him mildly and steadily said, "Sir, this is an instance that we are always most violent against those whom we have injured," a remark that should have silenced even Johnson; but "he was irritated still more by this delicate and keen reproach, and roared out another tremendous volley which one might fancy could be heard across the Atlantic." Yet if he had proclaimed his hatred for Americans ten times as often and ten times as loudly, Americans would still religiously dine at the *Cheshire*

Cheese and sit in the seat of the scornful lexicographer. Johnson's great and tender qualities were never eclipsed, and have never been denied. He would melt in the most unexpected way. He would conquer by noble yielding, but he would not be beaten by blows. When after long contention he was being worsted he had resource to what Boswell calls "some sudden mode of robust sophistry," as thus: "My dear Boswell, let's have no more of this; you'll make nothing of it. I'd rather have you whistle a Scotch tune"; or, warmly, "Nay, sir, if you will bring in gabble I will not speak another word with you, upon my honour I will not." To such dismissals there was no answer. In one story there is an almost pathetic hesitation on the Doctor's part whether he should be angry or not. He decided to be angry, and the result was the famous quarrel and reconciliation scene with Beauclerk. The topic, you remember, was Hackman's murder of Miss Ray, and the scene ends thus:

A little while after this the conversation turned on the violence of Hackman's temper. Johnson then said: "It was his business to *command* his temper, as my friend, Mr. Beauclerk, should have done some time ago."

Beauclerk: I should learn of *you*, Sir.

Johnson: Sir, you have given *me* opportunities enough of learning when I have been in *your* company. No man loves to be treated with contempt.

Beauclerk: (with a polite inclination towards Johnson): Sir, you have known me twenty years, and however I may have treated others, you may be sure I could never treat you with contempt.

Johnson: Sir, you have said more than was necessary.

VI

Johnson's violence was frequently of a kind which no man could regard without a certain awe and pity or without an increase of respect for the melancholy giant to whom life, after all, presented many a dark riddle and many a mood of despair. Only a few months before his death occurred, at Oxford, that startling conversation in which he showed his temperamental fear of dissolution and his difficulty in accepting the orthodox consolations.

Dr. Johnson surprised him not a little by acknowledging, with a look of horror, that he was much oppressed with the fear of death. The amiable Dr. Adams suggested that God was infinitely good.

Johnson: That he is infinitely good as far as the perfection of his nature will allow I certainly believe; but it is necessary for good upon the whole that individuals should be punished. As to an *individual*, therefore, he is not infinitely good; and as I cannot be *sure* that I have fulfilled the conditions on which salvation is granted, I am afraid I may be one of those who shall be damned. (Looking dismally.)

Dr Adams: What do you mean by damned?

Johnson (passionately and loudly): Sent to hell, sir, and punished everlastingly.

Dr Adams: I don't believe that doctrine.

Johnson: Hold, sir; do you believe that some will be punished at all?

Dr Adams: Being excluded from heaven will be a punishment; yet there may be no great positive suffering.

Johnson: Well, sir, but if you admit any degree of punishment there is an end of your argument for infinite goodness simply considered; for infinite goodness would inflict no punishment whatever. There is no infinite goodness physically considered; morally there is.

Boswell: But may not a man attain to such a degree of hope as not to be uneasy from the fear of death?

Johnson: A man may have such a degree of hope as

to keep him quiet. You see I am not quiet, from the vehemence with which I talk; but I do not despair.

Mrs. Adams: You seem, sir, to forget the merits of your Redeemer.

Johnson: Madam, I do not forget the merits of my Redeemer; but my Redeemer has said that he will set some on his right hand and some on his left—— (He was in gloomy agitation, and said): I'll have no more on't.

VII

I have but played with the subject of Johnson as a talker. My impulse on sitting down with Boswell's book open, and pen in hand, is simply to transcribe. Indeed, one's sympathies are with the man who so annoyed poor Goldsmith by exclaiming: "Stay! Stay! Toctor Shonson is going to zay zomething." The interrupter is still laughed at, yet his behaviour crystallises Johnson's extraordinary ascendancy in conversation. Men did listen to him like that. Honest Michael Moser wanted so badly to hear the Doctor that he would not have one of his remarks quenched. That Johnson's talk should have been transmitted to us in its spirit and letter, with unrivalled abundance, is one of the miracles of literature. Young readers often ask where their reading should begin. Where can it begin more auspiciously than in Boswell's wonderful book, so British, so spacious, so suggestive and amusing! The *Life* may be compared to a great intellectual terminus from which lines of thought and inquiry radiate in every direction. Let Macaulay's words clinch the matter: "Homer is not more decidedly the first of heroic poets, Shakespeare is not more decidedly the first of dramatists, Demosthenes is not more decidedly the first of orators, than Boswell is the first of biographers."

[*September* 2, 1904.]

BYGONE GUINEAS

I HAVE spent an amused and amazed hour in looking over the writings which first brought me the joys and guineas of journalism. If I recall them it is only because they represent a typical and familiar door to newspaper work: the Turnover door. What is a turnover? A turnover is an article on a casual topic that turns over a page. A certain old-established evening paper which, for the sake of effective disguise, I will call the *Traveller*, prints a turnover every evening. It has printed one every evening for more years than I know, and for each it pays a guinea. Ten years ago it was printing my own lucubrations with commendable frequency. How ingenious and literary I felt them to be, these airy discourses on things in general! The turnover may range over the whole world of fancy, whim, and topical bric-a-brac. You may write a turnover on anything outside the subjects on which the journal itself must deliver news or opinions, provided you are not too learned, or too literary or too serious. You may enlarge on Character or on Candlesticks; you may develop the serious side of Punch and Judy, or the comic side of the Alphabet.

My first turnover, a rather weakly thing, was called *Small Happiness*. Its appearance in the *Traveller*, however, was quite a large happiness. It led off with a story of Lord Eldon (I hope it was Lord Eldon), who, on the morning after going with some friends to see a very dull play, was told that one of the party had regretted the barrenness of the evening. "Barren!" cried the judge. "Did he not see the gaslights flashing on the backs of the lobsters as we drove past the fishmongers' shops?" A good story, I think, but after my first paragraph there is a painful falling off. However, I am interested to come on a

scene which I seem to have witnessed in Doctor's Commons:
a costermonger couple, man and wife, wearily and amusedly
watching a young man who hovered nervously about the
door of the Vicar-General's Marriage Licence Office.
That quaint old precinct, so familiar to Dickens, has now
been improved out of knowledge, and the touts in uniform
who offered you matrimony in the street no longer give
spice to St. Paul's Churchyard. After a rather shameless
digression to Horace: I find myself quoting a nameless
Tottenham Quaker, who used to say very sympathetically
of Paley, whom he had known in his youth, "Dost thou
know what was Dr. Paley's *summum bonum*? Chief good,
thou knows? On a rough winter's night, when the wind
is howling and the snow falling outside, to sit beside the
fire with a foot on each hob, roasting chestnuts in a
grate." I then wax learned on the intimate delights of
great men, and appear to have known, or believed, that
Voltaire's *summum bonum* was to sit in an armchair before
the fire stroking a long, black, writhing Persian cat. I
end on no higher note than a popular song in which it
was advised:

> O let the world spin
> Like a buzz-top of tin
> Till all the good people go dizzy;
> But the sign of a man,
> Deny it who can,
> Is a knack of taking things easy.

The almost dissipated variety of the topics on which, in
our thirst for fame and guineas, we enlarged in those eager
days gives me a sense of bewilderment. Here, for example,
is a learned trifle about coffee, which it pleased me to
represent as a highly intoxicating liquid on the faith of
Brillat-Savarin, who, it seems, once saw in London—"sur
la place de Leicester"—a coffee drunkard who had nearly

wrecked his constitution, but had at last disciplined himself
to take only six cups a day. This article is followed, in
my collection, by a discourse on new clothes, entitled
Nips for New, in which I find myself relying to a painful
extent on Goldsmith's relations to Mr Filby, and Malvolio's
cross-garters. Incidentally I give off the following dubious
reflection:—"Depend upon it, no one but a philosopher
or a fool can triumph over the small awkwardness of a
new suit." *Wanted, a Lexicon*, is an attempt to classify
railway travellers, and, incidentally, a plea for a trained
casuist to formulate the ethics of the window-strap. *The
Reign of Cleverness* had not, I hope, any inspiration in
the vanity of a budding journalist. I find myself observing,
apropos of the ceaseless spread of culture, "A learned
peasantry is a frightful thought," and then breaking into
an original parody of Goldsmith (these were the days of
the *Yellow Book* and large paper editions):

> Ill fares the land, to hastening ills a prey,
> Where books accumulate and crops decay.
> The "younger men" may grow, the "fogies" fade,
> And "larger" paper please a larger "trade,"
> But spare this epitaph on England's pride—
> When Hodge got culture agriculture died.

Thus sagely we set up our bogies and knocked them down
again for a guinea. Yet one did not write turnovers for
the *Traveller* lightly: it was youthful, serious, and fine.

Is Anything Ugly? was another essay caught out of the
air. It is a masterpiece of transition. "Jine your flats,"
was a Yankee's advice, and half the art of a "turnover" is
in jining one's flats. My tutor in turnovers, ingenious
and successful L——, used to write down on a sheet of
paper every conceivable story or reflection that might be
worked into a given T.O. He then studied how he might
"jine his flats." I was a year behind him in experience,

but the following example of "flat-jining" strikes me as
passably nimble. It almost merits an index:

The ancient respectability of ugliness is indicated in
that Cymric legend which tells how three men, and three
only, escaped the battle of Camlen, in which King Arthur
received his mortal wound. They were the Strongest Man,
the Beautifullest Man, and the Ugliest Man.   The U. M.
escaped through the awe he inspired in all who met him.
It may be conjectured that he was the direct ancestor
of that Mrs. Conrady on whose surpassing ugliness
Charles Lamb wreaked his whole vocabulary of admiration.   For unredeemed and irremediable ugliness in a
face is a worshipful thing.   Thoroughness tells here as
elsewhere, and hence there is, it must be admitted, a great
gulf between a Mrs. Conrady and, say, that Mr Job
Bottles, stock-broker, whom Matthew Arnold slightingly
immortalised as a man "with black hair, a fleshy nose,
and a camelia in his button-hole."   But then Matthew
Arnold probably never saw Mr Bottles' face after a sharp
rise in Brighton A, or when he was fulfilling the purposes
of a charity dinner.   The records of personal plainness
are, indeed, bright with conquest and compensation,
and a happy indifference to its penalties.   Paul Scarron,
who was a prodigy of ugliness, used to liken himself
to the letter Z, and entertain his readers with an account
of a complicated arrangement of pulleys with which
he professed he was wont to take off his hat.   Scarron
knew that his ugliness was but a sauce to his good wit,
and, indeed, physical imperfections are often as useful
in enhancing graces of mind and character as the Brighton
house-smoke is in making a Turner sunset when, carried
out to sea by an October breeze, it hangs in yellow
glory over the Channel.

Let no one imagine that our turnover erudition argued us
to be very learned.   But we knew how to beat it up.

There are two newspaper stalls behind the Royal Exchange with a wide asphalted space in front of them. In how many fateful luncheon hours have I made a sweeping approach to these stalls, with the eye of a hawk, for the *Traveller*, which was always piled in front of the open counter. Was *it* in? I could distinguish one of my own titles on the front page some yards away. If it were not there the curve of my swoop continued; but if it were, it was joyfully broken, and the *Traveller* became *sauce piquante* to my lunch. So have I rejoiced to descry *The Hearth*, *The Umbrella*, *The Value of Dirt*, *Our Small Ignorances*, *Mesopotamia* (not the country but "that blessed word"), *Men's Modes*, *Street Antipathies*, *Freaks of Fame*, *The Friendship of Places*, *The Vocabulary of Colour*, *Mermaids*, *On Making Believe*, *Bombast*, *The Magic of Names*, *Best Clothes*, and, to name a title which perhaps is descriptive of all, *A Little Learning*. I tried once to make a corner in turnovers. I wrote one called *Jack*. It was a study of the name and its connotations, and was full of minced learning. Then I sent in *Harry*. And then *Tom*. When these had been printed I began to scent an assured private income. I wrote *Peter*, and *Peter* appeared. Then *Bill*, and *Bill* had his day. But the *Traveller* now became restive. It printed *Dick*, but when I sent in *Jim* it very properly kicked. I believe I have *Jim* still.

[*September* 9, 1904.]

DAN LENO

IT needs no courage or jugglery of speech to say that Dan Leno was a genius. It is merely by habit that we narrow this term to men who are masters in art, literature, music, and research. Genius has been defined as the "dint of the inimitable." The man who in any calling or accomplishment adds something to all that effort can attain has genius. Dan Leno had genius. Let anyone call up the scene and atmosphere of one of his performances; and then shut his eyes, and remember and compare; and he will see that Dan Leno brought something upon the stage that was not in his song, or in his talk, or in any of his nameable qualities; not even in his humour. None of these really distinguished him from others. Behind all lay a unique quality to which one cannot put a word. However, Dan Leno's genius came from the recesses of his character rather than from the recesses of his talent. There was an extraordinary issue of sympathy from the little man. Who can forget that dry, rushing, pleading, coaxing, arguing voice, hoarse with its eagerness, yet mellow with sheer kindliness and sweetness of character?

I do not think that the subject-matter of Dan Leno's humour counts. In result it bears no comparison with Mr. Dooley's. It has none of that penetrating and abiding quality. In print it is vulgar with the vulgarity of the music halls, but on Leno's lips all that was consumed as by fire. The sordid things of life—poverty, debt, domestic jars— lost their hurt under his ingenuities and catastrophes of candour. In describing the house he had bought (*Buying a House*) he said: "When you look through the side window the view is obstructed by trees. Well, they have been trees, but they're not now; they've been split. They're planks; in fact, it's really a bill-posting station." But

I am chary of quoting Leno, because this must do him injustice. His humour depended on its delivery; it was a lightning gift from man to man; an exquisite, reckless, irresistible fandango of fun round the little foibles of some familiar character—a doctor, a waiter, a shop-walker, a beefeater—yet so loosely tethered to its subject as to be free to indulge in any number of irresponsible drolleries of speech, verbal contortions, and what not. The unifying quality was the man's amazing rapidity and gusto. He drowned drollery in drollery, he annihilated thought; he seemed to absorb all the earnestness in the house and use it before our eyes to make us laugh. And there was nothing merely expert in his rapidity; the expertness was there, but it was the rapidity of expertness in the temperature of kindness.

This abounding kindliness and explosive frankness gave to all Leno did its supremacy. Dozens of music-hall singers used the same comic material, but no one approached him in the art of buttonholing an audience, say, rather, in the fact of loving it. The tone of sympathy, of privacy, never left his voice. He was for ever making a clean breast of it, and beginning again in a new frenzy of confidence or warning. In all of which you felt that he was only acting with the stream of his character, that he was indeed the kindest and most ebullient of men, and a delicious observer. When he appeared as a scrawny female, bent on marrying Jim, will-nilly, he indulged in the following reflections:

He's so kind—so different from my fust husband. Oh, I've been married before, girls. Yes, I'm a twicer. My first husband was a Spaniard. When he was cross, *oh!* the way he used to look at me, with *his black eyes and dark olive skin.* Oh, *girls*, beware of olive skinners.

This may be ordinary music-hall fun, but Leno made it great. He made it great by his intensity; not the false intensity of emphasis, but the emphasis of truth and intimate telling. When he warned girls—and what loyal directness he threw into the word "Girls"—to beware of olive-skinners, his preoccupied concern for all the girls in London who might be in danger from olive-skinned lovers so dominated the verbal joke as to enhance it electrically.

Leno's drollery was always less than Leno. A small boy might have invented much of his nonsense, but only a great artist and a good man could have made the heart laugh with it. In his song *The Jap*, he said he had been to Japan as a tea merchant, but the man he bought the plants of made a mistake and gave him rhubarb. Of course, he couldn't sell it, so he tried to pass it off as "a kind of new season shou-shou." A boy might have said "shou-shou"; there was no attempt to be more Japanese than the "Jap," to coin a clever word that the audience could not have coined. He just rapped out "shou-shou," and the house crowed like a child. But when a little later he began a preposterous love episode by saying, with his inimitable air of making things clear, "One morning I was watering the shou-shou . . ." everyone roared with gladness. You see little in this? Ah, but you were not there. Though humour is the simplest of human things, it is the subtlest to describe.

The truth is that Leno's jokes were not produced, they just happened, and that even when they came so fast that a prairie-fire of laughter swept the house. He was always driving on to some insane urgency ahead, or stopping to get himself—and us—out of some weird and imbecile muddle. His understanding with his audience was the essence of his success, and he knew this so well that he was capable of playing with it. What a triumph was his fuss of incredulity when he affected to see in our faces a blankness at his casual mention of Mrs. Kelly. "You see"—he was still the scrawny female declaring her long passion for Jim:

You see we had a row once, and it was all through Mrs. Kelly. You know Mrs. Kelly, of course—Mrs. Kelly—Mrs. Kelly? You know Mrs. Kelly? You must know Mrs. Kelly. Good life-a-mighty! don't look so simple. She's a cousin of Mrs. Nipletts, and her husband keeps the what-not shop at the—oh, you must know Mrs. Kelly. Everybody knows Mrs. Kelly. Set down in print these words bear no more relation to Leno's delivery of them than an artist's easel, brushes, and lay-figure do to a masterpiece. The changes of demur, surprise, protest, unbelief, petulance, which he imported into the repetitions of Mrs. Kelly's name cannot be described, yet they were far less remarkable than the substance and expansion which he gave to Mrs. Kelly's existence. As her name recurred not only she, but all her kin and acquaintance, all her twopenny-halfpenny dealings and disputes, seemed to take shape, until—as the repetition in changing keys went on—whole breadths of London rushed into view, all the flickering street corners on Saturday nights, all the world of crowded door-steps and open windows, where Mrs. Kelly is Mrs. Kelly. Nothing would do until we had acknowledged a life-long acquaintance with Mrs. Kelly, and upon this immense confirmation of her existence came overwhelming mirth, having its seat in sheer sunny realisation of life. Only Leno could do this. How often, under his spell, have I seen two thousand people rock with laughter like a little family. For such a gift there is no word but genius, and for its extinction none but calamity.

[*November* 11, 1904.]

THE RIFF-RAFF OF SPEECH

A RACING-TIPSTER sorrowfully admitted, the other day, to a County Court judge, that "mugs" are scarce just now. He hoped to be in funds when the "mug season" arrived in April. The newspapers are for ever throwing into view these inside words—words, that is to say, that belong to corners of life more or less exclusive. Not that "mug" is a recondite word; few people can be strangers to it. But one of the fascinations of slang words is that they are, so to speak, skeleton keys with which one can unlock unaccustomed doors. Indeed, the best definition of slang is, perhaps, that of Professor Barrère: "A conventional tongue with many dialects, which are, as a rule, unintelligible to outsiders." A man who will take the trouble to acquaint himself with the origin and history of every slang word which meets his eye in the newspapers must soon be possessed of much curious information. Slang dictionaries are numerous, the best of them all being, of course, the monumental seven-volume work of Henley and Farmer, entitled *Slang and its Analogues*. This is an expensive work, but an admirable abridgment of it in a single volume has just been published by Messrs. Routledge under the title of *A Dictionary of Slang and Colloquial English* (7*s*. 6*d*.). This will serve most investigators, and it is free from the grosser words which abound in the more comprehensive work.

On the derivation of "mug," a fool, the dictionary before me throws no light. The most searching inquiry, as frequently as not, fails to trace a slang word to its source. "Mug," however, is associated with a kind of stupidity in the schoolboy's verb "to mug," i.e. to study, in neglect of games. One might imagine a connection between "mug," in its sense of a raw fellow, and the old Yorkshire word "mug," a sheep without horns. By a transposal of sense "mug" is used as a verb, in the sense of to rob or swindle, though no one would talk of "mugging a mug." The same thing occurred with the old and very widely used word "gull," which has been used to describe both the victim and the trickster. "Pigeon" is in the same case. It is defined as "a dupe, a gull"; but pigeons were also sharpers who, during the drawing of the lottery, used to lurk about the Guildhall. "As soon as the first two or three numbers are drawn, which they receive from a confederate on a card, ride with them full speed to some distant insurance office, before fixed on, where there is another of the gang, commonly a decent-looking woman, who takes care to be at the office before the hour of drawing; to her he secretly gives the number, which she insures for a considerable sum: thus biting the biter." I confess that the operation of this swindle, as explained by Francis Grose, escapes me, but the general sense is plain. The harmless Guildhall pigeons of to-day have thus a rather shady ancestry. For the most part the pigeon was the victim. He fell to the "rook" at the gaming table. Hence Thackeray's *Captain Rook and Mr. Pigeon.*

It seems possible that "mug" and "juggins" are allied by long-past association with drink and fuddlement. Juggins, applied to a person easily imposed upon, came into general use not much more than twenty years ago, though in Lancashire it is of older date. In his *Sybil* Disraeli introduced a miner named Juggins, who was imposed upon by his employer:

"Comrades," continued Nixon, "you know what has happened; you know as how Juggins applied for his balance after his tommy-book was paid up, and that incarnate nigger, Diggs, has made him take two waistcoats." Now the question arises, what is a collier to do with waistcoats?

Juggins, by the way, is a real surname, and it may be that its mere sound has in some obscure way suggested its new meaning, just as in the north of England the surname Jobson has lent itself to mildly humorous treatment, and Simpkins, Tompkins, etc., elsewhere.

It is inevitable that the world which abounds in ways that are devious and tricks that are vain should be a hotbed of slang. There language is literally a device for hiding one's meaning—from outsiders. It falls into two divisions, consisting of cant words which will never be anything else, and dictionary words degraded to cant meanings. Of cant words proper there are many thousands, and the inquirer will not often search Henley and Farmer's pages vainly for their elucidation. In this Abridgment no fewer than three closely-printed columns are filled with synonyms for thief or swindler. Many of them are curious in a high degree. An "amuser" was a thief who threw dust or snuff in the eyes of his victim before robbing him. An "anabaptist" was a thief caught in the cat and ducked in a horse-pond. A "Billy Buzman" is a pocket-handkerchief stealer. A "blue-pigeon-flyer" strips lead from roofs. A "cork" is a bankrupt. A "purple dromedary" is not quite so obviously a bungling thief as a "finger-smith" is a pickpocket. A "groaner" operated at funerals. A curious word for highwayman was "high toper," or "high toby." Toby meant the road. A "toby-concern" was a highway robbery. "Toby" was used exclusively of robbery on horseback, though a footpad was sometimes called a "lowtobyman." A passage in *Don Juan*, the Shooter's Hill episode, comes to mind in this connection. Other varieties of thieves are jilters, legs, magsmen, Newgate-birds, parlour-jumpers, queer shovers, and reader-merchants. A "swimmer" was a thief who escaped prosecution before a magistrate by offering to join the Navy. A "Tyburn-blossom" was picturesquely defined by Grose as "a young thief, who in time will ripen into fruit borne by the deadly never-green." A leader of thieves, or a thorough-paced thief, was honoured with the title of "upright-man." A still more impudent perversion was the use of "workman" for a thief. A "ziff" is a young thief: what else could he be?

Money, which we are told is the root of all evil, has received, alike from thieves and honest men, a bewildering variety of names. Thus money in general is known as:

The Actual	King's Pictures
The Blunt	Lurries
Coliander Seeds	Moss
Dirt	Nonsense
Evil	Oil of Angels
Flimsy	Pieces
Gilt	Rowdy
Hard	Spondulicks
Iron	Tin
John Davis	Wad

The slang of specific sums is interesting in a sordid way. For a million pounds not many terms can ever have been needed, and Henley and Farmer give only one. It is a "marigold"; £100,000 is a "plum"; £1,000 is a "cow"; £500 a "monkey"; £25 is, of course, a "pony"; £10 is a "double finnup," or a "long-tailed finnup"; £5 being a simple "finnup." This word appears to be a Yiddish form of the German "fünf"; £5 was long known as an "Abraham Newland," from the celebrated Bank of England cashier. To "sham Abraham" was to forge a note. When we descend to smaller sums, the variety of names is greater. A sovereign has been rechristened a "glistener," a "gold-finch," a "mousetrap," a "new hat," a "quid," a "remedy," a "stranger," and a "thick 'un." Ten shillings is known in some circles as a "half-bean" and a "smelt." A five-shilling piece was once known as a "coach-wheel," and is still sometimes called a "cart-wheel." The names for a shilling include "blow," "bob," "generalise" (why "generalise"?), "north-easter" (from the letters N. E. on New England coins of Charles I), "Manchester sovereign," and "peg." A sixpence, now called in slang little else than a "tanner," has been a "tester," a "tizzy," a "lord-of-the-manor," a "bender," and a "cripple." The origins of some of these words can be seen or guessed. Thus a sovereign was called a "skin," because it was good filling for a skin, or purse. A shilling was known as a "breaky-leg," and the origin becomes plain when breaky-leg is found to have meant strong drink.

I have but skimmed a little backwater of my subject. I wish I could conclude by quoting the whole of the late Mr. Henley's powerful ballade *Villon's Straight Tip to all Cross Coves*, in which the thief's calling is reduced to its miserable result in his own "lingo." It is a master-piece in its way, and the moral lesson is complete as in any tragedy of "wine and women." Here is the first stanza and the "moral":

> Suppose you screeve? or go cheap-jack?
>   Or fake the broads? or fig a nag?
> Or thimble-rig? or knap a yack?
>   Or pitch a snide? or smash a rag?
>   Suppose you duff? or nose and lag?
> Or get the straight, and land your pot?
>   How do you melt the multy swag?
> Booze and the blowens cop the lot.

> .   .   .   .   .

>   It's up the spout and Charley Wag
> With wipes and tickers and what not.
>   Until the squeezer nips your scrag,
> Booze and the blowens cop the lot.

With the *Dictionary* this cry of an all but penitent thief can be read with ease, and perhaps with profit.

[*February* 3, 1905.]

LITERATURE OF A CRIME

THE remarkable conversation which recently took place between Mr. William Archer and Mr. Churton Collins on the human interest in murders is but another example of the appeal which such events often make to the literary mind. Probably the supreme crime of this sort is the murder of Mr. William Weare by John Thurtell and Joseph Hunt, near Elstree, Middlesex, in the evening of October 24, 1823. It is nothing less than astonishing to see how this particular tragedy crops up in books of the highest interest. I propose to exhibit these literary associations. But first I must tell in plain words the story which gave pause to Lamb's epistolary pen, impressed by one of its incidents the imagination of Edward FitzGerald, drew Sir Walter Scott out of his path to the spot where it was enacted, gave Lord Lytton a thrilling chapter in *Pelham*, inspired a poem hardly inferior to the *Dream of Eugene Aram*, and added a word to Carlyle's vocabulary.

In 1823 there flourished in Bow Street a small tavern called the *Brown Bear*, much frequented by sporting men and gamblers. These were the great days of the prizering, and the enormous interest which Thurtell's crime excited throughout the country was partly due to its connection with the sporting life of the period. John Thurtell and his brother Thomas were frequenters of the *Brown Bear*. They were young men of good position, sons of a Norwich alderman. John had served his country, and had seen the storming of San Sebastian. He had then settled at Norwich as a manufacturer of bombasin, but he cheated his creditors of £400, and came to London. Here he entered into business with his brother in 1821, but he appears to have been more addicted to gambling at the

Brown Bear than to transacting business in their Watling
Street premises, which, in January, 1823, were burnt down
under suspicious circumstances. Meanwhile, his experiences in the half-lit "hell" at the *Brown Bear* were such
as to cause him great embarrassment and to rouse his
temperamental desire to be revenged on his enemies. In a
word, he was fleeced. Just when his eyes were opened,
and when he might, perhaps, have given up gambling as
a sorry mode of life, his "friends" added to their cruel
depredations their yet more cruel kindness. They arranged
a bet for him on a "sold" prize-fight, by which he won
£600. This success wedded him to the life he was leading,
but unfortunately it did not extirpate his hate or curb his
extravagance. One of his associates was a Mr. William
Weare, who had chambers in Lyon's Inn—a fact which a
mock-Catnach ballad of the time perpetuates in a singularly
unpleasant stanza. Thurtell always said that Weare had
been one of his despoilers. He deliberately planned to
murder Weare, and to rob him of a considerable "private
bank" which he was known to carry in the pocket of an
under-waistcoat. It is clear that flat robbery was not so
much Thurtell's object as revenge and the getting back of
the money which he considered Weare had improperly
won from him. Indeed, he seems at this time to have
formed a programme of vengeful murder, which was to
include at least two other men, one being the Mr. Barber
Beaumont who was now prosecuting his brother Thomas
in the matter of the Watling Street fire.

The imminence of this prosecution made it necessary
that the Thurtell brothers should conceal themselves. In
this they were assisted by a friend whom they trusted, a
Mr. Probert, a spirit-dealer, who had a cottage in Gill's
Hill Lane, near Elstree, in Hertfordshire, off the St. Albans
Road. Thurtell, in the awful deliberations of a murderer,
decided on this place as the scene of his intended attack on

Weare. He had visited Probert there many times, and knew the surrounding lanes and fields intimately. On the evening of October 23, Thurtell and Hunt met Weare at Rexworthy's Billiard Rooms, and Thurtell asked him if he would go down to Elstree for two or three days' shooting. Weare accepted this invitation, and on the following day, in his chambers at Lyon's Inn, packed up some clothes in a green carpet bag, together with a back-gammon board, and equipped himself with a double-barrelled gun. While he was thus engaged Thurtell and Hunt were buying a pair of pocket-pistols at a pawnbroker's in Marylebone. This done, they returned .to the *Coach and Horses*, in Conduit Street, where they met Probert. Thurtell now remarked to Probert that he had a mind to go down to his cottage that night, and then revealed his intention to "do" Weare. He said he would drive down to Elstree in a gig, and would pick up Weare, by appointment, at the end of Oxford Street. He wished Hunt and Probert to drive down in another gig, and if they passed him, Hunt was to wait at a certain spot not far from the lane leading to the cottage.

Nothing is more extraordinary than the way in which the murder was regarded as a mere incident of the journey, and of the evening's employments. Thus Hunt got down from his gig in Oxford Street, and bought a loin of pork with a view to supper at Elstree. At the end of Oxford Street he remarked: "This is the place where Jack is to take up his friend." They drove on, and four miles from London overtook Thurtell, who was driving a dark grey horse. Hunt said: "There they are; drive by and take no notice. It's all right. Jack has got him." From this point the two gigs were lost to each other. Hunt and Probert, dismounting a little beyond Edgware, spent three-quarters of an hour drinking brandy-and-water at the *Artichoke Inn*. It was then nearly eight o'clock, and the

F .

two men were mystified by Thurtell's failure to overtake them. The fact was that Thurtell and Weare had passed them without their perceiving it. When Probert had dropped Hunt at the place where he was to meet Thurtell, and, pursuing his drive alone, had entered Gill's Hill Lane, he was amazed to see Thurtell approaching him on foot. Thurtell asked him where Hunt was, adding that he did not want him now, as he had "done the trick." I will not tell all that is known of the murder. Weare had begged, then fled, for life; and it needs little imagination to picture the horror of that dark lane, heavy with the scent of autumn leaves, which flew from the feet of pursuer and pursued, and the struggle in the light thrown by the lamps of the gig.

Nor will I describe the ghastly doings of the night, the removal of the body, and the sinking of it in a pond close to Probert's cottage, and the braggings, whisperings, and rustle of banknotes that roused fearful suspicions in the mind of Probert's wife, who, looking from her window at midnight, witnessed part of the unholy business. Next morning the three men found to their terror that respectable neighbours had heard pistol shots and groans. They dragged the body out of the pond and placed it in a sack, after which Thurtell and Hunt drove away with it, and flung it into a marsh. The clumsiness and recklessness of the murderers proved their undoing. Hunt actually had the callousness and folly to array himself in a suit of Weare's clothes taken from the green carpet-bag. A stain on the gig cushion which they feared Probert's stable-boy would notice, was to be accounted for by saying that they had flung a hare upon the seat. But discovery was on their heels. The pistol which Thurtell had left in the lane, and for which they had sought vainly with a lantern, was picked up by some labourers, who found also every trace of a deed of blood. And yet there was nothing to prove absolutely that a murder had been committed. Of the victim there was no trace. But suspicion deepened every hour, and it was established that a stranger had been seen in Thurtell's gig and had mysteriously disappeared. Probert, Hunt, and Thurtell were arrested as a precaution, and inquiry became hot. Hunt, in his alarm, told the magistrates where the body would be found, and Probert, who had never known Weare, though he knew what his fate was to be, made a clean breast of the facts. In the result he was called as the principal witness against Thurtell and Hunt, who were tried for the murder at Hertford Assizes. They were found guilty and both condemned to death.

The excitement produced by the trial was almost unprecedented. The roads to Hertford were crowded with vehicles. In London the Catnach Press broke down in its efforts to supply the story of the crime to its patrons. James Catnach is said to have made over £500 by the event. His premises in Little Earl Street, St. Giles's, were so besieged by hawkers that, in despair of supplying them from his own four presses, he set other printers to work. Toiling night and day at the hand-presses, he managed to turn out over half a million copies in eight days. In the hurry and confusion it was impossible to check deliveries, and the printers whom he employed not only learned his methods but cheated him by selling thousands of the copies he had employed them to print. The *Death Verse* on the broad-sheet began thus:

> Come, all good Christians, praise the Lord,
>   And trust to Him in hope.
> God in His mercy, John Thurtell sent
>   To hang from Hertford gallows rope.
>
> Poor Weare's murder the Lord disclosed—
>   Be glory to His name:
> And Thurtell, Hunt, and Probert, too,
>   Were brought to grief and shame.

In all ways the trial fully answered expectations, for Thurtell made a speech from the dock, which, though flowery and hypocritical, was well conceived. He pointed to his services as a soldier, and claimed that he had all a soldier's instincts towards his fellow-men, whatever might have been his errors. But he marred his speech greatly by reading to the jury many pages from the *Percy Anecdotes*, instancing the dangers of circumstantial evidence.

Interest in the crime was not all sordid, as is proved by the wonderful verses written by the Rev. John Milford. The chief incidents are introduced in a way that is the reverse of crude, while the sensational element is raised to the weird. These verses, which first appeared, I believe, in *Raw's Pocket Book*, are as follows:

THE OWL

(Scene: The Cottage in Herts.)

Owl, that lovest the cloudy sky,
      In the murky air
      What saw'st thou there,
For I heard through the fog thy screaming cry?
      "The maple's head
      Was glowing red,
And red were the wings of the autumn sky;
      But a redder gleam
      Rose from the stream
That dabbled my feet as I glided by."

Owl, that lovest the midnight sky,
      Speak, oh! speak,
      What crimson'd thy beak,
And hung on the lids of thy staring eye?
      "'Twas blood! 'twas blood!
      And it rose like a flood,
And for this I scream'd as I hurried by."

Owl, that lovest the cloudy sky,
      Again, again,
      Where are the twain?

"Look while the moon is hurrying by:—
  In the thicket's shade
  The one is laid—
You may see through the boughs his moveless eye."

Owl, that lovest the cloudy sky ,
  A step beyond,
  By the silent pond,
I heard a low and moaning cry.—
  "By the water's edge,
  Through the trampled sedge,
A bubble burst and gurgled by:
  My eyes were dim,
  But I look'd from the brim,
And I saw in the weeds a dead man lie."

Owl, that lovest the midnight sky,
  Where the casements blaze
  With the faggots' rays.
Look, oh! look! What seest thou there?
  Owl, what's this
  That snort and hiss—
And why do thy feathers shiver and stare?
  "'Tis he, 'tis he—
  He sits 'mid the three,
And a breathless Woman is on the stair."

Owl, that lovest the cloudy sky,
  Where clank the chains,
  Through the prison panes,
What there thou hearest, tell to me.
  "In her midnight dream
  'Tis a woman's scream,
And she calls on one—on one of three."
  Look in once more
  Through the grated door.
"'Tis a soul that prays in agony."

Owl, that hatest the morning sky,
  On thy pinions gray
  Away, away!
I must pray in charity;
  From midnight chime,
  Till morning prime,
Miserere, Domine!

An interesting circumstance about these lines is that they were the last which that strange being, Beau Brummell, copied into his poetry album.

But the most famous literary relic of Thurtell's trial is to be found in the works of Thomas Carlyle. His use of the word "gig" as a synonym of respectability had its origin in the following dialogue between counsel and a witness:

What sort of person was Mr. Weare?

He was always a respectable person.

What do you mean by respectable?

He kept a gig.

Carlyle's fierce sardonic humour seized on this, and whenever he was storming at respectabilities and unrealities gigs were not far from his mind. The principal allusion is, I think, in his essay on Richter, but "gigs" were henceforth among his literary properties, and he uses them even in the grandiose conclusion of his *French Revolution*:

Metal Images are molten; the marble Images become mortar-lime; the stone Mountains sulkily explode. RESPECTABILITY, with all her collected Gigs, inflamed for funeral pyre, leaves the Earth; not to return save under new Avatar . . . For it is the End of the dominion of IMPOSTURE (which is Darkness and opaque Fire-damp), and the burning up with unquenchable fire of all the Gigs that are in the Earth.

By "gigmanity" Carlyle named all the forces of respectable, smug, *laissez-faire* society.

In consideration of the aid he had given to the magistrates, the sentence of death on Hunt was commuted to transportation, and this led to an incident which greatly struck Edward FitzGerald in his quiet life of books and boats at Woodbridge. Thurtell's passion for revenge, which had been directed against all who had taken his money, did not extend to the accomplice who had, by giving information, helped to take away his life. He expressed a strong wish to have Hunt's company on the night before his execution. This it was that moved Fitz-Gerald to admiration. In a letter to Fanny Kemble, written more than fifty years after, he says:

I like, you know, a good Murder; but in its place.

> The charge is prepared; the Lawyers are met—
> The Judges all ranged, a terrible Show.

Only the other night I could not help reverting to that sublime—yes!—of Thurtell, sending for his accomplice Hunt, who had saved himself by denouncing Thurtell—sending for him to pass the night before Execution with perfect Forgiveness—Handshaking—and "God bless you—God bless you—you couldn't help it—I hope you'll live to be a good man."

As a fact, Hunt behaved so well in his life in Australia that he rose to be the chief constable of a considerable town in the interior. On the day after this meeting between the two men Thurtell stood on the scaffold. It is said that his fate appealed so strongly to his friends of the prize-ring that a serious plan was laid to rescue him at the last moment, and that this would in all probability have been carried out if the sum of £500, necessary for the hire of men, could have been obtained from Thurtell's family. As it was, much pity was lavished on the condemned man at the end, a waste scornfully referred to by Sir Walter Scott in his *Journal*. Yet Scott himself, in 1828, took considerable trouble to visit Gill's Hill Lane, and we have his comments on the crime which had made it infamous. In a madcap letter to Bernard Barton, in which Charles Lamb complains of ennui, emptiness and "numb, soporifical goodfornothingness," he jerks forth these exclamations, apropos of nothing: "I can't distinguish veal from mutton—nothing interests me—'tis twelve o'clock, and Thurtell is just now coming out upon the New Drop," adding that he cannot elicit a groan or a moral reflection on the event. No more can I; yet the story seemed worth the re-telling.

[*June* 2, 1905.]

THE YORK COLUMN
And the Man on it

I AM asked to explain the York Column, and the request is reasonable. The "marrow" of the Nelson Column puzzles thousands of visitors to London, and probably just as many Londoners. Who is this man, with the lightning-conductor growing out of his head, who looks down on the Horse Guards Parade and on the Westminster group of public buildings? Whose effigy is thus raised as high as the national hero's? Why was it erected, and was it deserved?

The last question is partly disposed of by the fact that the Duke of York's Column was erected many years before Nelson's. Its scale has therefore only an accidental equality with that of its renowned neighbour. The two Columns can be seen in picturesque relation to each other from the west end of Carlton House Terrace, and I commend this little-known view to the camera brotherhood. One cannot help thinking that the York Column ought to be the Wellington Column. Then the figures of our greatest sailor and greatest soldier would be conspicuous side by side. As it is, the Nelson and York Columns pair well in the fact that the one stands for the Navy and the other for the Army. For it was to perpetuate the memory of the Duke of York's services as Commander-in-Chief that the Column in Carlton House Terrace was erected, and not—as has been irreverently said—that the Duke might be put beyond the reach of his creditors. Moreover, the second son of George III, in spite of faults, was a good servant to the State and a good fellow. And though he was not a Wellington, it fell to him, as commander of the expedition to the Netherlands, to give young Wellesley his first chance on the field. But that is another story.

For making a complete mess of the Flanders campaign the Duke was appointed Commander-in-Chief, an office which he held, with one well-deserved suspension, for the rest of his life. On the whole, he was a good Commander-in-Chief, and it cannot be forgotten that it was under his rule at the Horse Guards that England vexed Napoleon in Spain and crushed him at Waterloo. Unfortunately the Duke's administration was marred by a great scandal. In the careful obituary sketch of the Duke which he contributed to the *Gentleman's Magazine*, Sir Walter Scott did not spare to condemn the Mrs. Clarke episode. The Duke had allowed his mistress to suggest and procure promotions in the Army over which he should have exercised the purest control. A hot Parliamentary inquiry brought about his resignation in 1809. It was recognised, however, that he had been the dupe of an artful woman, of whose trafficking with officers he had certainly no knowledge, and in 1811 he was re-appointed Commander-in-Chief with the approval of the public, who liked him. Princes of the blood are never among those who are forbidden to look over a hedge.

And so there he stands, 124 feet above censure and Carlton House Terrace. One turns from the dimness of judgment to the candle-light of anecdote. Scott tells a story which is more than biographically interesting. At one of the Duke's dinner-parties a young officer entered into a dispute with a Lieut.-Colonel upon the point to which military obedience ought to be carried. "If the Commander-in-Chief," said this young officer, "should command me to do

a thing which I knew to be civilly illegal, I should not
scruple to obey him, and consider myself as relieved from
all responsibility by the commands of my military superior."
"So would not I," returned the gallant and intelligent
Lieutenant-Colonel. "I should rather prefer the risk of
being shot for disobedience by my commanding officer,
than hanged for transgressing the laws and violating the
liberties of the country." The Duke had been listening,
and he now gave judgment. "You have answered like
yourself," he said, "and the officer would deserve both to
be shot and hanged that should act otherwise. I trust all
British officers would be as unwilling to execute an illegal
command, as I trust the Commander-in-Chief would be
incapable of issuing one."

Outside the Army the Duke was a burly royalty about
town, and, generally speaking, a good-humoured volup-
tuary. He haunted the Watier Club, founded by his
brother, the Regent, where the dinners were exquisite and
the gambling ruinous. He uttered at Newmarket the
words, "a shocking bad hat," which, for some mysterious
reason, are immortal. The origin of one of the Duke's
friendships is told by Captain Gronow. When the notor-
ious Count Montrond was making his way into London
Society the Duke asked: "Who the deuce is this
Montrond?" "They say, sir, that he is the most agreeable
scoundrel and the greatest reprobate in France." "Is he,
by Jove! then let us ask him to dinner immediately." But
the Duke's more serious companions were men like Alvanley,
Beau Brummell, Charles Greville (who managed his racing
stud), and Sir Thomas Stepney, to name only a few in
the circle which he drew round him at the Stable Yard at
St. James's Palace. Thus environed and encouraged, the
Duke soon owed £200,000. We hear of him being so
tipsy one night that he had to be blooded. The world
went very well then.

In his later years the Duke of York was not taken seriously as Heir Apparent, for his life was rendered "bad" by a combination of punctuality at the Horse Guards and lateness at the table. Yet he was hopefully planning and building York House (now Stafford House), when dropsy laid him on his death-bed. From his room in Rutland House, in Arlington Street, which had been lent to him, he could hear his workmen's hammers. The death of the Duke was sincerely mourned, and the burial at Windsor was carried out at night, with all usual pomp. At the graveside many distinguished people took severe colds, a consequence which Lord Eldon escaped by standing (with acute reluctance) inside his hat.

In 1831 the Army projected a monument to their lost leader. Carlton House had just been demolished, and Carlton House Terrace had been built in its two ranges. The space between these was to have been filled by a fountain formed of the eight columns of the portico of Carlton House. Before this plan was executed the idea of a grand entrance into St. James's Park from Pall Mall was mooted and preferred. The Carlton House columns went to support the portico of the National Gallery, and the new approach to the Park was selected as the site of the Duke's monument. The York Column is a plain Doric pillar standing on a granite pedestal. The height of the column, exclusive of Westmacott's bronze statue, is 124 feet. The statue itself is $13\frac{1}{2}$ feet in height. The Duke is represented in a robe, with a sword in his right hand, and in his left one of the insignia of the Order of the Garter. The cost was £26,000.

Away east the Duke of York has a less perpendicular monument. The £72,000 which the Crown received by the sale of the palace he was building went to purchase Victoria Park.

[*August* 3, 1906.]

THE FALL OF THE LEAF

TO go out to see a prophet and to be stopped by a reed shaking in the wind is perhaps an ordinary experience. I went to see Turner's paints and brushes, now being shown at the Tate Gallery, but the memory of that afternoon will always be of the plane leaves falling in unending, silent shower against the dark traceries of Henry the Seventh's Chapel. London was one great guest-house, full of sunshine and strangers. The char-à-banc drove up and departed, or waited idly under St. Margaret's Church, while Big Ben boomed over Royal Westminster. In one unending shower, without haste and without dallying, the plane leaves fell on the grass, and still the gold above and the gold below seemed the same. The falling leaf is a mystery. You see it fall, but with all your watching you do not see it quit the tree. The leaf also—like the bird and like the man—has the instinct of secrecy in death. Whole companies float down, but whence they come is still an inference: the tree is there and the leaves are here. The leaves fell slowly against the dark traceries of Henry the Seventh's Chapel, wherein much has fallen in four hundred fallings of the leaf. Gone is the vast gold cross and the golden statue of the Virgin that was to have watched over the Founder's tomb for ever; gone the great altar on which the figure of the dead Christ lay in angelic keeping; and gone the monks who were to sing for the peace of Henry's careful soul "as long as the world shall endure." And the type of all this change was the leaf, seen as a yellow falling flake in the twilight of the Abbey walls.

"The fall of the leaf" is now an autumn phrase, but when Henry the Seventh's chapel was building it was the very name of the season. Autumn is the only season which we know by a Latin-derived name. Spring, summer, winter are Old English, and "the fall of the leaf," or "the fall," belongs to this set of names. So early as 1543 we have Roger Ascham enumerating the seasons as "spring-tyme, somer, faule of the leafe, and winter." In Shakespeare we hear the gardener say of the unhappy Richard:

> He that hath suffer'd this disorder'd spring,
> Hath now himself met with the fall of leaf.

There is a very pretty use of the word "fall" in the Milkmaid's Mother's Answer in *The Compleat Angler*:

> The flowers do fade, and wanton fields
> To wayward Winter reckoning yields.
> A honey tongue, a heart of gall,
> Is fancy's Spring, but sorrow's *Fall*.

The truth is that the word "autumn" was slow to commend itself to the common people, and was long regarded—nay, is still regarded—as a "fine" word. In Lincolnshire and other places the season is constantly named as "the back end." In Yorkshire and other counties I believe the word "fall" is still frequently heard. The common idea that "fall" is an Americanism is quite wrong. The early emigrants took the word to America, where it has flourished to this day. It happens that we have a record of this fact. In one of his letters to the Free Society of Traders, a letter bearing the Quakerly-expressed date of "16th of 6th month, 1683," William Penn describes the Pennsylvania seasons and begins: "First of the fall, for then I came in." Autumn is a beautiful word, but it is curious that we have preferred it to Fall, which is the most expressive name that human lips could bestow on the "season of mists and mellow fruitfulness." "Spring" is not so expressive, for the springing of the earth's verdure and flowers is not so perceptible as the fall of the leaf. "Fall" is autumn in the act.

Of all the seasons, autumn has the secret of moving our subtlest perceptions and memories. I have always thought that Tennyson exploded the perfect adjective on autumn when he called its fields "happy" at the moment when he wrote of the "divine despair" which the sight of them evokes in the human heart:

> Tears, idle tears, I know not what they mean,
> Tears from the depths of some divine despair,
> Rise in the heart, and gather to the eyes,
> In looking on the happy Autumn fields,
> And thinking of the days that are no more.

An autumn landscape lifts and burdens the heart equally, and this because it moves and enriches the spirit in a peculiar degree. It is the crisis of the year. The earth's endowment and doom are seen together. More than at any other time we divine that secret of creation whose figurative story could not have been told save in terms of autumn. "Let the earth bring forth grass, the herb yielding seed, and the fruit tree yielding fruit after his kind, whose seed is in itself." Most of us, I believe, are strangely conscious of the spring in the autumn, and of the autumn in the spring. These seasons exchange their musics when they play on the human heart. Many a writer has asked the question which George Macdonald raised in his beautiful book, *Annals of a Quiet Neighbourhood.* "Can anyone tell me why it is that, when the earth is renewing her youth in the spring, man should feel feeble and low-spirited, and gaze with bowed head, though pleased heart, on the crocus; whereas, on the contrary, in autumn, when Nature is dying for the winter, he feels strong and hopeful, holds his head erect, and walks with a vigorous step, though the flaunting dahlias discourage him greatly? I do not ask for the physical causes: those I might be able to find out for myself; but I ask, Where is the rightness and fitness in the thing? Should not man and Nature go together in this world which was made for man—not for science, but for man? Perhaps I have some glimmerings of where the answer lies. Perhaps 'I see a cherub that sees it.'" Literature is full of such passages. I recall one in the pages of Obermann, that super-sensitive annalist of feeling and nuance.

We shall never understand man's account with his destiny until we recognise that he is not merely doomed to mortality, but is organised for it, and is in love with the idea. The spectacle of Nature's decline reminds him of his latter end, only to restore and harmonise his spirit, and to infuse it with a joy too deep for dance or song—the joy of wisdom and understanding seeking the language of prophecy. The finest poetry ever written is the poetry that should fill us with despair, but we pass it down the ages as the vibrations of the master chord. I do not here speak of the idea of death transmuted into the hope of another life. Mortality itself, the grandiose certainty of the end, the fall of the leaf, the extinction of the flame, the turning down of the empty glass: from all these ideas of the evanescence of all things man has not vainly fled, but in the strength and bitterness of his soul he has drawn from them his supreme music and the last luxury of thought. We are not saddened by these statements of our end any more than by Nature's annual statement of her own. When Horace bade Posthumus remember death's inexorable rage, and ran through the catalogue of human farewells:

> Your pleasing consort must be left,
> And you of villas, lands, bereft,

he did no violence to friendship and to human feeling by the unction and cumulative emphasis of his warning,

not even when he added to the picture of the cypress tree
darkening over his friend's tomb the mocking postscript:

> Then shall your worthier heir discharge
> And set th' imprison'd casks at large,
>   And dye the floor with wine,
> So rich and precious, not the feasts
> Of holy pontiffs cheer their guests
>   With liquor more divine.

For the instinct of destruction lies so deep in the human
heart that we find a secret satisfaction in our own. I have
always felt that this matchless Ode derives no small part
of its power from the vision flung across it of the Adriatic
hoarsely surging in its autumn mood. It is because
autumn evokes a profound sympathy with our own
mortality that its appeal transcends those of the other
seasons. Man's unconquerable soul is made happy by
his ability to feel the deep things of life deeply, rather
than by his ability to deduce from them any material good
or final advantage. And this is the lesson of the falling
leaf.

[*October* 16, 1908.]

YORICK COMES TO TOWN

THE sudden making of a splendid name is inevitable
in war, punctual in science, rare and astonishing in
literature. Shakespeare, so far as we know, did not wake
one morning to find his name on every lip. Nor did
Milton, nor our greatest poet since Milton, Wordsworth.
But Byron's fame grew in one London night, and Charlotte
Brontë's with hardly less of magic. Neither event can

quite compare with that which suddenly and indelibly inscribed on the roll of English literature the name of Laurence Sterne.

It is doubtful whether London has ever, before or since, put herself out to recognise and welcome an utter stranger as she did in the first week of March, in 1760, to greet the "tall, thin, hectic-looking Yorkshire parson," who had just become known as the author of a five shilling book called *The Life and Opinions of Tristram Shandy, Gentleman.** published, not in London, but in York. Sterne had been fairly dragged up to London by his friend Stephen Croft, and it appears that neither of them knew, when they were in the stage-coach, that a furore of social welcome awaited Sterne. They slept in Chapel Street, Mayfair, at the house of Nathaniel Cholmley. Sterne was forty-seven, and knew that he had produced a work of genius. And now he lay in London hearing only the watchman's droning call, and maybe the yells of the Mohock tribe. But as soon as possible next morning he stole away from Chapel Street to Dodsley's shop in Pall Mall. To Dodsley he had consigned some copies of the book, but not many, because the whole York edition consisted of only a few hundred copies. Sterne threaded his way down to Pall Mall, and walking with throbbing heart into the famous Tully's Head book shop, whence had come Johnson's *Vanity of Human Wishes*, he inquired how *Tristram Shandy* fared. He was overjoyed to hear that a copy of the book could not be had for love nor money. Soon afterwards, by chance, or on a suspicion of his whereabouts, Croft and Cholmley came to Pall Mall, and there found Sterne deep in a momentous bargain with Dodsley, but coolly haggling over an odd £50. With their help the contract was signed, and presently Sterne was skipping about in his room in Chapel Street,

---

* *The Life and Letters of Laurence Sterne* by Lewis Melville (Stanley Paul & Co.).

G

and announcing to his friends that he was the richest man in Europe.   In a sense, he was.

In one respect, Sterne's issue from Yorkshire was inferior to Charlotte Brontë's.   The author of *Jane Eyre* used no guile to capture London, and her fame descended on her head as the sunshine from heaven.   Sterne we now know —and Mr. Melville makes this amusing—was in reality equipped with the impudence and artifice of the most accomplished modern "boomster."   It is known that his introduction to the social and literary worlds of London was given him by Garrick.   Well, the great actor's first knowledge of Sterne's existence, and of his authorship of a book called *Tristram Shandy*, was derived from a letter written to him from York by Kitty de Fourmantelle, commending Sterne to his notice, and, unfortunately, it has been discovered that this letter was dictated to Kitty (Yorick's first flame) by the parson himself, whose own draft is in existence, and is now in the possession of Mr. John Murray.   The device is capable of repetition and I will quote this precious epistle for the benefit and advantage of whomsoever it may concern:—

York, January 1st, 1760.

Sir,—

I dare say you will wonder to receive an Epistle from me, and the subject of it will surprise you still more, because it is to tell you something about Books.

There are two Volumes just published here, which have made a great noise, and have had a prodigious run; for, in two days after they came out, the Bookseller sold two hundred, and continues selling them very fast. It is the *Life and Opinions of Tristram Shandy*, which the Author told me last night at our Concert he had sent up to London, so perhaps you have seen it; if you have not seen it, pray get it and read it, because it has a great character as a witty, smart Book, and if you think

so, your good word in Town will do the Author, I am
sure, great service. You must understand he is a kind
and generous friend of mine, whom Providence has
attached to me in this part of the World, where I came
a stranger—and I could not think how I could make
a better return, than by endeavouring to make you a
Friend to him and his performance; this is all my excuse
for this liberty, which I hope you will excuse. His name
is Sterne, a gentleman of great Preferment and a Pre-
bendary of the Church at York, and has a great character
in these parts as a man of Learning and Wit; the graver
people, however, say 'tis not fit for young Ladies to
read his Book, so perhaps you'll think it not fit for a
young Lady to recommend it; however, the Nobility
and Great Folks stand up mightily for it, and say 'tis a
good Book, tho' a little tawdry in some places.

I am, dear Sir, your most obedient and humble servant.

The art of the thing almost justifies its artifice.

Human nature being what it is, we may be sure that men
like Johnson and Goldsmith, who had starved and fluc-
tuated, and men like Gray and Walpole, who had waited
and finessed, did not join in the instant acclamations of
Sterne! Shandy! Yorick! that filled the town. It is not
probable that Johnson asked for the new Shandy Salad
at the Mitre or that Goldsmith put money on the horse
Tristram Shandy, though it ran in an Irish steeplechase.
Everywhere there were shrugs and sore hearts in the
literary world, and a growing ebullition of parodies, jeers,
and hostile criticism, all of which are sufficiently reflected
in Goldsmith's chapter in his *Citizen of the World*, entitled:
"The absurd taste for obscene and pert novels, such as
Tristram Shandy, ridiculed." In the annals of literary
jealousy and misapprehension, this essay is a *locus classicus*.
Its concluding words would be admirably punitive and just

but for the simple fact that Sterne was a genius and an immortal! Yet Goldsmith's criticism applies so well to Sterne's imitators, and, for that matter, to all writers who try to be high-fantastical without having the right to be so, that it is worth quotation:

As in common conversation, the best way to make the audience laugh is by first laughing yourself; so in writing, the properest manner is to show an attempt at humour, which will pass upon most for humour in reality. To effect this, readers must be treated with the most perfect familiarity; on one page the author is to make them a low bow; and in the next to pull them by the nose: he must talk in riddles, and then send them to bed in order to dream for the solution. He must speak of himself and his chapters, and his manner, and what he would be at, and his own importance, and his mother's importance, with the most unpitying prolixity: now and then testifying his contempt for all but himself, smiling without a jest, and without wit possessing vivacity.

Johnson spoke grudgingly of Sterne, but Gray, who was in London at the time, beheld the triumph—and wrote: "Tristram Shandy is still a greater object of admiration, the man as well as the book. One is invited to dinner, where he dines, a fortnight beforehand. His portrait is done by Reynolds, and now engraving. Dodsley gives £700 for a new edition, and two new volumes are not yet written; and to-morrow will come out two volumes of sermons by him." Meanwhile, Sterne himself, revolving on his Shandean pivot, became a little dizzy with adulation. He poured out his heart in letters, not to his wife at home, but to his dear friend, Kitty de Fourmantelle, then at York. To her he writes: " I have the greatest honors paid and most civility shown me that were ever shown from the great; and am engaged already to ten Noble Men and Men of fashion to dine. Mr. Garrick pays me all and more honor than I could look for. I dined with him to-day, and he has promised numbers of great People to carry me to dine with them." *Tristram Shandy* was something quite new, and the man being remarkably like his book—a likeness which he took abundant care to cultivate—was new also, and Society ran after him and talked about him for much the same reasons as it now runs after and talks about Bergson. It did not understand his book, nor the man who wrote it, but it comprehended that Shandyism was the *mot d'ordre*, and Parson Sterne the man to invite to dinner and the theatre. Society, as it happened, had got hold of a good thing: for once it had assisted at the birth of genius. The Church itself, for some inscrutable reason, blessed its son's literary and personal vagaries. He was able to write to his adored Kitty: "Even all the Bishops have sent their compliments to me, and I set out on Monday Morning to pay my visits to them all."

Strange that the man who was welcomed to London with unexampled openness by bishops, peers, and the cream of society, should have ended his days alone and neglected, in Bond Street, eight years later. We all remember how little pity for that end was shown by Thackeray. The "coward," the "wretched worn-out old scamp," the "feeble wretch": these are the final epithets which the author of *Vanity Fair* bestows on the arch-sentimentalist who, in the hour of his triumph, was pouring out his jubilations, not to his wife, but, as we have seen, to a professional singer. During these eight years of his fame Sterne kindled the torch of his genius at flames not of his hearth. Mr. Melville will tell you all you can wish to know about Kitty de Fourmantelle, Mrs. Vesey, Lady P., and the all-pervading Eliza. To Thackeray, Sterne's philanderings and desertions seemed abominable, and it is certain that nothing can make them creditable. But that

Thackeray judged him harshly is now generally admitted. Sterne's own account of his mania for entanglement was this:—

> I must always have a Dulcinea in my head.... Having been in love with one princess after another almost all my life, and I hope I shall go on so till I die, being firmly persuaded, that if ever I do a mean action, it must be in some interval betwixt one passion and another: whilst this interregnum lasts, I always preserve my heart locked up—I can scarce find it to give misery a sixpence: and therefore I always get out of it as far as I can, and the moment I am rekindled, I am all generosity and goodwill again; and would do anything in the world either for or with anyone, if they will but satisfy me there is not sin in it.

And so, between his temperament and his sophistries, Yorick said and wrote and did things which in most men would go unpardoned   Thackeray boils with indignation over his letter to Eliza Draper, then returning to her husband in India, in which he pictures her as his future wife—he and she being both married. But this wild dream cannot be isolated from the *Journal to Eliza* as a whole, and what is the total character of these amazing letters? They are instinct with nervous disease, and with the semi-jocose, all-hopeless grasp after the sweets of life of a stricken and dying man   He stops at nothing in mawkish day-dreaming. Weakness has its false strength, and although the last look on life may be "longing" and "lingering" in most cases, there are others in which it is fevered and uncontrolled.

Without doubt, Sterne was one of the most strangely composed men who ever lived. He had the impulse to love without the power, and, as Mr Melville says, he never really loved a woman in his life. The pleasant misleadings of sentiment, the sense of "ships that pass in the night,"

the wayward and impossible magnetisms of the heart,
were to him as the breath of his nostrils. He was so much
an epicure of sympathy that he could never be done trifling
with the *hors d'œuvres* of life's banquet. But the human
heart is like a garden, in that it will harden and sour if it
is not dug deep and watered and aerated by the penetration
of strong roots. Sterne was for ever refining and arrosing
the surface of his heart, gathering frail blooms that quickly
faded. His heart was always in appetite, never nourished.
Almost to the last he was able to deceive himself and others.
When planning his *Sentimental Journey* he exclaimed to
a friend: "Praised be God for my sensibility! Though it
has often made me wretched, yet I would not exchange
it for all the pleasures the grossest sensualist ever felt"—
not seeing, or not acknowledging, that the true well-being
of the heart lies remote from either extreme. Such is the
diagnosis which reason and charity will make of the *Journal
to Eliza*. Here was a philanderer of fifty-four, married to a
jealous wife, picturing his future union with a young
woman of twenty-three, herself returning to a vigilant
husband in India. There is no ground for believing that
Sterne had compromised himself with Mrs. Draper.
"Sensibility" running amuck is the spectacle. He sees
and writes of everything in terms of Eliza. Thus, from
his Yorkshire vicarage:—

I am in the vale of Coxwould, and wish you saw in
how princely a manner I live in it—it is a Land of Plenty
—I sit down to Venison, fish or Wild foul—or a couple
of fouls—with Curds, and Strawberries and Cream and
all the simple clean plenty which a rich Vally can produce
—with a Bottle of wine on my right hand (as in Bond
Street) to drink your health—I have a hundred hens and
chickens about my yard—and not a parishioner catches
a hare, a rabbit, or a trout—but he brings it as an Offering.
—In short, 'tis a golden Vally—and will be the golden

Age when You govern the rural feast, my Bramine [his jocose pet name for Eliza], and are the Mistress of my table, and spread it with elegancy and that natural grace and bounty with which heaven has distinguish'd You.

What is this but the language of sentiment insured against risks by a previous mutual understanding—itself bordering on a delicately mutual cynicism? Any other reading of it seems impossible. Sterne's passionate venison and rapturous "curds" may well have suggested to Dickens the Pickwickian chops and tomato sauce.

And thus it was that the man who in 1760 came to London, with all his wit and novelty and tentacular pseudo-sympathies, to fascinate society, came hither for the last time in 1768, broken in health, beset by chagrins, unwarmed by natural affections, though yearning for the touch of his daughter's hand. In lonely lodgings in Bond Street poor Sterne prepared himself, as he could, to take the journey that is never "sentimental." His death has been compared to Falstaff's. It would have been witnessed by no human eye but for an accident. A party of his friends, which included Garrick, Hume, the Dukes of Grafton and Roxburghe, and a few others, were dining together, when someone mentioned Sterne's illness. On an impulse they sent a footman round to Bond Street to inquire his condition. The landlady bade the fellow go upstairs to see for himself. He entered the room just as Yorick was dying. He watched his last struggle and heard his last words: "Now it is come!" In a dreary field of the dead, unknown to most Londoners, near the Marble Arch, the dust of Laurence Sterne lies, under a stone inscribed with many words, including these: *Ah! molliter ossa quiescant*. No man had more need of rest, for none was more restless in life.

[*Undated: about* 1909.]

THE SOUL OF THE READY WRITER

I LIKE to read about the ready writers whose mission it has been to strike a bliss upon the day, the week, the month, and not to faint by the road. But such information is rare. The newspaper essayist, the dramatic critic, the feuilletonist, these can leave no substantial monuments of their desiccated toils; they have left only slight tracks in the crowded ways of life and literature, on which new footsteps have fallen, and on which more than one little epoch has shed effacing leaves. Here and there, by a chance, of self-revelation or of outside reminiscence, we glimpse the evening and the morning that made the Ready Writer's day, his alternations of furore and fatigue, his spectres of exhaustion, his happy renewals of strength, and a little of his standing with the readers to whom he gave the daily bread of culture. It is just this all-important relationship between the one who wrote and the thousands who read that eludes us most. Sainte-Beuve put it admirably when he wrote in 1850 about several of the old veterans of the *Journal des Débats*, the *Globe*, and other Paris journals. After affirming that the critic is only the secretary of the public, who divines the thought of the world, and therefore expresses himself in terms which come to be obscure because they have all the little omissions and anticipations of bygone intimacy, he writes:

I maintain that in re-reading the old journals and the critical articles which had most success, we never find more than half the article in print: the other half was only written in the minds of the readers. Imagine a printed page of which we read only one side; the *verso* has disappeared, it is blank. Add that this *verso* which would complete it is the disposition of the public at the time, the part of the redaction which they brought to it, and which often was not the least intelligent, least active. It is this disposition itself which, in order to be accurate, we should have to restore to-day, when we judge the old critics, our predecessors.

All this is true, and it explains why there is no humane and anecdotal literature of journalism comparable to the literatures of law and medicine.

It is to talk of Sainte-Beuve himself, the greatest of the Ready Writers, that I have set out; but let me approach him along the path on which I have started. Just now I am concerned with certain brief passages in the *Causeries du Lundi*. Behold an event, too ripe to be very sad, has given Sainte-Beuve the idea of gossiping about the bygone men of his own craft, men who entertained the public with their pens. For on the 11th of the month of February, 1850, had died, at the age of eighty-three, M. de Feletz,

> an amiable and witty old man, who, under the forms of an exquisite politeness and a perfect social urbanity, concealed a strong character, clear and consistent opinions, much practical philosophy; a safe and a happy man who had preserved, in spite of the habits of a critic and an ordinarily pungent wit, a kindly and warm heart, an extreme delicacy in friendship.

This M. de Feletz had been once an active writer on the *Journal des Débats*, then called the *Journal de l'Empire*. Touched by the passing away of this venerable reviewer and essayist, Sainte-Beuve wishes to pay a tribute to his memory and to that of the old school of critics to which he belonged. He wishes to think of their toils, to look curiously at their work, and to vision, if possible, the public they entertained. It is the best kind of "shop" that he will talk in next Monday's *Constitutionnel*. For although these men flourished long before his day, Sainte-Beuve is not unprovided with matter. That restless and

delightful curiosity which thrust him among living men
not less constantly than among books had led him in good
time to call upon M. de Feletz and to persuade him to talk
about his old confrères on the *Journal de l'Empire*.   It is
from his notes of that interview that Saint-Beuve now con-
structs his "Monday chat," and it is from his preliminary
cogitations that he evolves the remarks which I have
already quoted on the difficulty of resuscitating the relations
between an old critic and his vanished readers.

The outstanding figure in Sainte-Beuve's essay, the best
realised, is that of Geoffroy, the rough and learned dramatic
critic of the *Débats*.   His early career had been scholastic.
After the Reign of Terror he returned to Paris, being then
nearly forty.   Bertin, the editor of the *Débats*, wanted a
dramatic feuilleton, and he pitched on Geoffroy as its
writer.   The appointment was a great success.   This
middle-aged professor threw himself into the dramatic
mêlée with gusto, and the *Débats* treated him handsomely.
He had a good salary, a box at every theatre, and a carriage
to take him there, "not to mention the rest."   His articles
enjoyed a prodigious vogue.

> This Geoffroy was a strong and vigorous nature.
> There are, for modern journalistic criticism, two filiations,
> two distinct lineages; the one honest, scrupulous,
> impartial, born of Bayle; the other, born of Fréron.
> Geoffroy was sprung from this latter line, but he singu-
> larly raised it, at least at his first beginnings, by the
> energetic, though even a little coarse, boldness of his
> good sense.   He was, properly speaking, the creator of
> the dramatic feuilleton; but he also broached all sorts of
> subjects. . . .

It is clear that Geoffroy's charm for the public had to
do with his hard hitting.   With writers like Roederer,
Chénier, and the Abbé Morellet he quarrelled to the top
of his bent.   One would like to see some of the sentences

he wrote when his blood was up. "Incredible abuse" is Sainte-Beuve's phrase, as he looks over them.

I seem to hear one of those third-rate characters in Molière, one of these good bourgeois who let themselves go, and who are not wanting in *jaw*, as they used to say at the time. "It enfeebles literary criticism," Geoffroy maintains, "to go seeking after roundabout ways of expressing faults which can be very clearly specified by a single word: applied to the person, this word might be an insult; applied to the work, it is the right word." And this word he immediately blurts out, without thinking any more of his distinction between the person and the work. "Some of my expressions," he says again, "appear to them ignoble and trivial: I would like to be able to find words still more capable of painting the baseness of certain things of which I am obliged to speak."

Having rather given one the idea that the words of abuse he *had* discovered were the results of earnest though imperfect search, and therefore presumably of calculation, this headlong Geoffroy immediately continues in this unexpected way:

My sentences are not the result of calculation, of a cold intellectual combination; they follow the movements of my soul; it is my feeling that gives me the tone; I write as I am moved, and *that is the reason why I am read*. In other words, Geoffroy justifies his abuse by declaring that he writes it in an uncontrollable temper? Sainte-Beuve archly comments: "We must admit that the man who feels like that, when he comes to deal a just blow must deal it vigorously." All this is excellent "shop." And I am reminded that Geoffroy makes a sudden and slightly comic appearance in another of Sainte-Beuve's essays. He was once moved to draw a picture of the Ready Writer's lot. "It is not a small matter," he pointed out to amuse the public three or four times a week; to call up one's wit at will, every day, and on all sorts of subjects; to treat the most serious things playfully, and always to insinuate a little seriousness into the more frivolous, continually to refresh a used-up stock, to create something out of nothing.

It is indeed not a small matter.

Perhaps Sainte-Beuve's most sympathetic description of a feuilletonist is that with which he opens his essay on Jules Janin. It is a delightfully cunning irrelevance. Janin has written a novel, and clearly it is not a very good novel. Sainte-Beuve therefore finds a way to dwell upon Janin the clever critic before coming to Janin the dull novelist. He represents him as a man of letters who has the worthy idea to turn aside from his feuilleton work, which to-day is and to-morrow is cast into the oven, to do himself the justice of writing a book and to give himself a little monument. To the book he will turn presently; meanwhile he would like to observe that "twenty years ago M. Janin formed a style and manner of his own, that he created a feuilleton which bears his stamp."

Those who have tried this profession (and I have been one of them for some time), and who know what periodical efforts it requires, will appreciate the degree of facility and spirit, the force of temperament (that is the word), which M. Janin needed to be equal to them for so many years without fatigue, without disgust, to work as easily and smoothly on the last day as on the first. . . . M. Janin, in amusing, finds his own amusement; he is evidently amused by what he writes: that is the surest way to succeed, to remain always in the humour and in practice. He gaily and light-heartedly sets about doing what would be a task and a drudgery to another. There he is, in that study, nay! in that pretty garret from which he writes, and which he has had the good

taste never to leave, like the bird in his cage. . . .   He
has made great demands on the imagination, on the chance
opportunities of the moment, on all the bushes at the
roadside; the bushes who have paid him back much.
M. Janin is a descriptive writer, whose strength lies
especially in the happiness and surprises of his details.
He has formed a style which, on his good days and when
the sun smiles, is lively, graceful, airy, made of nothing,
like those light and transparent gauzes which the ancients
call *woven air*.   Or, again, this ready, piquant, sparkling
style, served up to the minute, resembles a fresh and
foaming sherbet that one takes in summer under the
trellis arbour. . . .   On an evening mist, on a passing
violinist, on a departing dancer, on a dying flower-girl,
he has written delightful pages, which deserve to live.
On Scribe, on Balzac, on Eugène Sue, on Théophile
Gauthier, on Méry, he has written rapid, delicately-
shaded criticisms, found on the spur of the moment,
which cannot be reproduced, which should be cut out,
isolated from their surroundings.

Such reading, I say again, delights me.   Why will not
some capable hand give us a book about the Ready Writers,
in which the life shall be depicted, in which the fierce smell
of the printers' ink shall prevail, and in which we shall,
as far as possible, recapture the writer's toil of the night
and the reader's smile of the morning?

Another comrade of M. de Feletz on the *Débats* was one
Dussault.   But of Dussalt's work de Feletz had spoken
cautiously.   This critic did not go to the bottom of things,
and would not commit himself.   Sainte-Beuve, too, remembers that Joubert said of Dassault: "His style is an agreeable
twitter of birds, in which one can discover no distinct
melody."   Then there was Hoffmann.   These are unfamiliar names.   But herein lies the interest, and, if you
will, the mild tragedy.   These men, so little remembered,

delighted their generation. Hoffmann had lyric and dramatic gifts; he could construct little dialogues and comedies to lighten his articles when he chose. And he was conscientious.

> He used to read everything he had to discuss, an essential condition, and yet rarely found in the critical profession. . . . Afflicted by night with insomnia, he read continually, and being gifted with a capacious memory, he forgot nothing he had once read. An accurate, sincere, and scrupulous mind, possessing the art of delicate irony, he lacked an elevated sense of poetry. He betrayed the deficiency when he had to speak of Chateaubriand's *Martyrs*, of Guizot's *Shakespeare*, of the first Odes of M. Victor Hugo.

To this Sainte-Beuve adds, to the scandal, I fear, of my Scottish readers:

> One might find, however, some just remarks in what he says of Walter Scott's novels, which excited much enthusiasm at the time, an enthusiasm that would listen to no limitations. He analyses and very capably disentangles the true causes of the interest they rouse; he points out what that supposed and so much talked-of historical fidelity amounts to. The positive portions of Hoffmann still deserve to be read. He was an enemy of infatuations and all kinds of charlatanism, which is a true character and sign of the critic.

This sympathetic essay closes with a sketch of M. de Feletz himself, the urbane, delicately satiric "critic of good society." Of him we read:

> He could make himself understood without being explicit. The grain of salt came in at the end, in a quotation, in an anecdote. In his manner of ending, in the cast of his sentence, he had a certain motion of the head which we knew well; he had something of the Abbé Delille in prose.

In these glimpses of his environment and kinships, we have cast only sidelong glances of homage at Sainte-Beuve, the greatest of the Ready Writers, the most human and entertaining critic who ever put pen to paper. Of him hereafter.

* * * * *

A young man who feels he requires stimulus in the pursuit of knowledge will find it in merely submitting his mind to the influence of what has been justly called Sainte-Beuve's "passionate intellectual curiosity." Nor will he be the less charmed with the critic's independence, his lack of proselytising zeal. This great writer sets the mind in motion and floods it with serene and playful light, but he does not try to convert his readers. When he had issued sixteen volumes of his wonderful *Causeries du Lundi* he proudly remarked: "I have given no one the right to say 'He belongs to us.'" Again, in describing the successive phases of his intellectual development, he emphasises his habit of turning always on his own pivot:

In all these wanderings I never (save for a moment in the Hugo period, and when under the influence of a charm, forfeited my will, or my judgment, never pawned my belief. On the other hand, I understood so well both the world of books and that of men that I gave dubious encouragement to those ardent spirits who wished to convert me as one of themselves. But it was all curiosity on my part, a desire to see everything, to examine closely, to analyse, along with the keen pleasure I felt in discovering the relative truth of each new idea and each system, which allured me to my long series of experiments, to me nothing else than a prolonged course of moral physiology.

A moral physiologist, Sainte-Beuve approached a book as a man examining the thoughts of another man. He therefore desired to find out everything about the writer— his birth, training, habits, idiosyncrasies, weaknesses.

Only when he had collected every scrap of information about him, every *mot* or anecdote that lit up his personality, and had read his book in the light of this knowledge, and with sufficient regard to the spirit of his period, was Sainte-Beuve ready to put pen to paper. He then evolved a critical portrait—full, just, and entertaining—and submitted it to his readers. It was by the senaturalistic methods that he triumphed as a critic, and it was by his faithful industry and punctuality in providing Paris with one of these superb studies every week, during twenty years, that he takes his place as the greatest of Ready Writers.

Charles Augustus Sainte-Beuve had a sufficiently narrow escape of not being born. His father, a worthy and bookish Commissioner of Taxes at Boulogne, was fifty-two when he married Mlle. Augustine Coillot. This lady, the daughter of an Englishwoman who had married a Boulogne sailor, was past forty. Six months after the marriage M. Sainte-Beuve died, and it was on December 23, 1804, that his wife gave birth to the son who was to attain the highest honours in literature. It was from his father, whom he never saw, that Sainte-Beuve derived his intellectual qualities. "I was born," he says, "in a time of mourning; my cradle rested on a coffin. . . . My father left me his soul, mind, and taste." He explains that it was in the family books, filled with his dead father's marginal notes, that he acquired the inner meaning of the words learning and taste. Then came to him, as it comes to all young men of brains and aspiration, the years of doubt and conflict, of seeking and misgiving, of depression and difficult adjustment to the ways of the world. The story of this *Sturm und Drang* period is told by him in the fictitious *Life of Joseph Delorme*, prefixed to his early volume of poems. Joseph Delorme was young Sainte-Beuve, hovering between beliefs and anxiously seeking a way by which he could earn a living and yet be himself. The book was the *Sorrows of Werther* on a small scale, and personal to the young scholar, poet, and medical student who had the world before him. Long afterwards, in 1849, in the very first of his *Causeries du Lundi*, he recalled this period when writing about that eminent literary professor and journalist, M. Saint-Marc Girardin. In view of the correspondence now proceeding in this journal on the difficulties of character building, I quote at some length Sainte-Beuve's remarks on the malady of Chateaubriand and youth.

M. Saint-Marc Girardin's influence upon young men has been real, and deserves to be noted. An enemy of pomposity and of grand airs, he has helped to unmask many vices of declamation in vogue in his time; he has pricked many a bladder. But he is above all one of those who have most contributed towards curing the young generation of the malady of René. What is this malady? . . . René's evil is disgust with life in isolation, of thinking oneself misunderstood, of despising the world and the beaten tracks, of judging them unworthy of oneself, of esteeming oneself the most desolate of men, and of loving one's one melancholy; the last stage of this evil would be suicide. Few people in our days have committed suicide in comparison with the number of those who have threatened to do so. But we have all, at a certain time of our lives, been more or less attacked by René's malady. M. Saint-Marc Girardin, who was always exempt from it, has hit off its disastrous effects and its absurdities; he has spared no pains to make young men disgusted with it, and he has succeeded. He has not ceased to repeat in every tone, in a tone of mockery as well as in a tone of affection: "Do not think yourselves superior to others; accept common life; do not sneer at petty morality, it is the only good one. Stagyre's demon is melancholy, or rather a want of energy and backbone

—it is the negation of the soul. In order to get away from it, esteem regular and simple habits, everyday duties and interests above all kinds of pleasures. Adopt a profession, marry, and get a family. There is no demon, indeed, though it were the demon of melancholy itself that will dare to face the presence of little children." In such and still better terms (for I am obliged to abridge) has M. Saint-Marc Girardin for nearly eighteen years been preaching marriage to the younger generation, regularity in the beaten tracks, the love of the high roads: "The high roads," he exclaimed one day, "I will not speak ill of them; I adore them."

To which the young man of melancholy Twenty-Two may object: "What is this but to quench my dreams and put me into the street?" Sainte-Beuve (still the most human of critics) sees the other side, states it, and leaves the reader to digest and apply all these reflections. He proceeds:

I have said that M. Girardin was successful, too successful, indeed. The younger generation, or part of them, have become positive; they have given up dreaming; as soon as they are sixteen they think of their career and all that may lead up to it; they do nothing useless. The mania and the emulation of all the Renés and all the Chattertons of our time was to be a great poet or to die. The dream of the young wiseacres of to-day is to live, to be a prefect at twenty-five, or a delegate, or a minister. The evil has merely changed and shifted. That is what happens with all the maladies of the human mind which we flatter ourselves to have cured. They are repercussed, as they say in medicine, and others are substituted. M. Saint-Marc Girardin, who knows human nature so well, knows that better than we do.

Sainte-Beuve emerged (like the vast majority of young men) from the incandescence of the early twenties. His medical studies in Paris, to which he was bound, and from which he was about to break, became part of his strength. In him poetry and science were uniting to set a new attitude to literature. As a latter-day critic* has said: "The mystic in Sainte-Beuve was always side by side with the physiologist, the unflinching analyst, just as the poet was ever comrade to the critic. It is to this, indeed, that Saint-Beuve owes his pre-eminence, to this that is to be traced the fundamental secret of his spell." In 1824, the year of the death of Byron, the *Globe* newspaper was founded in Paris by M. Dubois, under whom Sainte-Beuve had won the History prize at the College of Charlemagne. The professor took his pupil with him to the *Globe* office, and gave him lessons in the art of writing. One day he said: "Now you know how to write; henceforth you can go alone." Encouraged and happy, Sainte-Beuve went ahead, and was presently entrusted with certain volumes of *Odes and Ballads*, which M. Dubois said were by "a young barbarian of talent." This was Victor Hugo. Sainte-Beuve was now in the swim—so much so that he shortly rose to the dignity of fighting a duel with M. Dubois himself. It would be tedious to explain how this came about; it is enough to relate that Sainte-Beuve appeared on the field of battle carrying a pistol in his right hand and an umbrella in his left. It was raining, and he explained that he was willing to be shot, but not to be drenched. Decidedly he had recovered from the "malady of René."

All through his life Sainte-Beuve eluded and annoyed those who desired to capture him for a party or a school. He desired a quiet life and liberty to change his mind when he saw reason to do so. In the stormy years of 1830 and onward this attitude more than once isolated him, or brought him into actual contumely, but never did he

* The late Mr. William Sharp, to whose memoir of Sainte-Beuve, prefixed to Vol. I of *The Essays of Sainte-Beuve* (Gebbings, 1901), I am indebted.

swerve from his love of letters and his desire to perfect himself as a student of life and literature. It was in 1849 that he embarked on the most characteristic enterprise of his life, those Monday Chats which appeared with such punctuality and with such unrivalled effect in the pages of the *Constitutionnel* and the *Moniteur*. I have already described Sainte-Beuve's critical method. Of his cloistral industry—Sainte-Beuve never married—we have a few glimpses. On Monday his article appeared, and on Monday he began the next. "I never get a day off," he declared. "About midday on Monday I lift up my head and breathe freely for about an hour. Then the door shuts again, and I'm in prison for a week." It may possibly seem to be a pleasant thing to be a brilliant critic and to be paid £640 a year for writing one article every seven days. Sainte-Beuve made of it an unsparing labour. He demanded to read and examine every book, letter, and document, published or not, which bore upon his subject. The whole allotted period was all too short for this process of saturation, and for the work of drawing the intended portrait. For, when all the facts were amassed and considered, there remained the task of using them in such a manner as to please both the scholar and the newspaper reader.

To please on the highest plane: this was Sainte-Beuve's task, and for twenty years it kept him to his room. Of that eyrie in the Rue du Montparnasse we have just a glimpse in the journal of the brothers Goncourt. They had gone to thank the great critic for a favourable review:

He lives in the Rue du Montparnasse. The narrow door was opened to us by his housekeeper. We were shown up into his bedroom, which, with its great book-cases, curtainless windows, and paper-laden table, might be that of a Benedictine monk thrown by fate into a common lodging-house.

To the Goncourts, too, we owe, a lively idea of Sainte-

Beuve's talk. Thus, in writing of one of the famous Magny dinners:

> There was to-day a battle royal round Thiers's History, and it must be confessed that we were unanimous in condemning him as an historian devoid of talent. Sainte-Beuve alone defended him. "He is such a charming man. He has so much wit and persuasive power! He lets you into the secret of how he carries parliament with him, and wins over a *député!*" This is the form of argument and the method of defence always adopted on all occasions by Sainte-Beuve.

In a word, Sainte-Beuve was all for human interest. He did not care to take sides; enough for him to look on and note the trait in the character, the point in the game. The Goncourts add another illustration:

> You have only to say to him "Mirabeau was a traitor," and he replies, "Yes, but see how he loved Sophie!" And then he will depict the passion felt by the traitor for his mistress. . . . He does this for everybody, and under any circumstances.

Sainte-Beuve began to break up in the early sixties. In 1865 he wrote: "I am of the age at which died Horace, Montaigne, and Bayle, my masters: so I am content to die." The Monday was fast approaching when Paris would have no article from Sainte-Beuve, no urbane and witty appreciation of a statesman's glory and weakness, a poet's Muse and mistress, to give it the taste for life. Yet Sainte-Beuve lingered on for four years, and was at work to the last. He died on October 13, 1869, in that house in the Rue du Montparnasse, in the room of bookcases and curtainless windows. A few biographical notes were found in his desk, ending with the words:

> *Devoted with all my heart to my profession as critic, I have done my utmost to be more and more a good and if possible an able workman.*

Here is a formula for happiness and success. Sainte-Beuve had long been an Academician, and therefore his burial called for the usual honours. But he had desired the simplest ceremony, and his wish was respected. He had perhaps little thought—perhaps no one realised—how his loss would be felt. But when it was remembered for how many years his wit, insight, learning, and style had produced their weekly masterpiece, how in depicting life he had cheered and entertained his fellows, all Paris rose in sudden sorrow. Ten thousand people followed him to his grave in the Cemetery of Montparnasse, where no words were spoken save these: "Farewell Saint-Beuve; our friend, farewell."

[*August* 13 *and* 20, 1909.]

THE NEW CANUTE

"THE local authorities are making every effort to attract visitors, and are being ably seconded by those who are promoting indoor entertainments."

Artemus Ward pronounced Shakespeare's tomb to be "a success," and to-day Shakespeare's "silver sea" may be conveniently described by the same word. When Shakespeare was alive, and for long after he was dead, the sea could not be called a success. It did little more than make us an island, inspire our poets and painters, and soothe by its colour and music the troubled heart of man. These were pleasing functions, but there was no money in them. As late as the year 1812 the Reverend William Clarke, a well-known divine and antiquary, was able to report to his friend Mr. Thomas Bowyer the cost of his lodgings at Brighton in these terms: "We have two parlours, two bed-chambers, pantry, etc., for 5*s.* per week." That is what the sea earned for a seaside landlady a century ago; to-day she may expect as much from the lights and cruet.

Later, the sea began to pay better on its merits, and it continued to do so down to the 'eighties of the last century. But all gold-fields attract too many diggers, and the time arrived when the vasty deep was found to be over-capitalised. Speculation had outrun discretion, and in some new watering-places, and the newer parts of some old watering-places, it was found that two mortgages did not last longer than one coat of paint. It was now that the beautiful commercial discovery was made that the way to make the mighty waters a paying concern was to suppress them as much as possible. The seaside, not the sea, must be developed. But the seaside promoter, having received the blessings of education, did not adopt the futile methods of Canute and Mrs. Partington. He neither ordered the waves to retreat nor attacked them with a besom, but instead he bustled to make us forget their very existence. If he could not stop the sea roaring, he could at least make the beach hum. He had grasped the great fact that people who are easily interested by the sea-shore do not leave nearly so much cash behind them as those who are with difficulty amused in the town. Moreover, the sea-loving people, as often as not, distributed themselves unprofitably along miles of cliff, and even overshot the rates. The problem was to concentrate them round the band-stand.

The first efforts to supersede the sea were, no doubt, small and tentative. One can smile at them now. If I remember rightly, they were directed largely to the establishment of monkey-houses and aviaries in all convenient spots. The Baths (where one skated) had their monkey-houses and aviaries, and at the entrance to the Skating Rink (where concerts ruled) appeared, as a matter of course, the seductive notice, "Monkey Houses and Aviaries."

The idea was meagre, but one sees that it was on the right lines. The invention of the penny-in-the-slot machine occurred about this time, and it came as a blessing to many a struggling coast. It is impossible to put a penny into a slot with one eye on the watery main. The act requires concentration, and when the visitor has completed it, and the little men in gloves begin to spar, or the fat hen lays one's fortune, Neptune may wave his trident as he pleases, but he must wait. It has been found possible to keep Neptune waiting indefinitely.

The seaside promoter has never faltered in this policy. His handicap (if I may apply a rather vulgar expression to a great crusade) was severe, for it cannot be denied that at many seaside places the sea is a conspicuous object. Moreover the older generation, who still bought the tickets, had to be educated out of their singular affection for the waves. There is little doubt that Dickens put back the development of our seaside resorts fully half a century when he made Paul Dombey listen to what the wild waves were saying. The people persisted in doing the same. The Amusements Committee knew perfectly well that this was a hoax; they had passed the whole winter by the waves, when they roared their loudest, and they knew that they had never heard them say anything.

Still, much could be done, and much was done. Piers were multiplied and lengthened. It was already beginning to be known that nothing diverts the mind from the sea more effectually than a properly-equipped pier whose shore end is well billed and whose marine end is fully licensed. Piers, however, have been known to defeat their object. People with good money in their pockets are still known to use a pier for watching the sunset at the very hour when the cinematograph shows are opening their doors and the M.C. is smoothing the creases out of his gloves. Aquariums, built underground, have great merits, for it has been discovered that the exhibition does not suggest the sea, and that if there is a proper equipment of punching machines and audiphones it is not necessary to maintain more than one fish to three tanks. Grottoes and Arizona silver mines, the larger the better, have been found most useful; but in these, as in all underground entertainments, the difficulty of maintaining the advertised percentage of ozone is apparent. Thus arose the noble idea of imitating the Eiffel Tower. From the top of an iron tower rising to nearly a thousand feet, the visitor can behold the sea to so much advantage (yet under strict surveillance) that he is likely to hold it cheap when he descends to its level, and, furthermore, he has obtained a bird's-eye view of the chief music palaces, dancing halls, cricket and tennis grounds, and sack-races; and he may even have watched with feverish interest, through a field-glass, the progress of an "open-air whist drive."

It is not possible in the limits of this survey to indicate the hundred and one different applications of the turnstile which are now employed to shepherd visitors. It may be that the business of working a seaside place is still in its infancy. After dinner, on a fine summer evening, the cliffs and beach are not so denuded of visitors as could be desired. True, thousands are packed into theatres and music halls, thousands are wedged into well-sunk band-pits, thousands more are being detained in boarding-houses by conjurers; but the members of the Amusements Committee are still distracted by the spectacle of middle-aged ladies and gentlemen who appear to be obsessed by a bygone conception of seaside pleasures. The beauty of the evening hour when

> . . . the mighty being is awake
> And doth with his eternal motion make
> A sound like thunder, everlastingly,

is a serious factor—the revenue from deck-chairs being

really negligible. Even quite young people often take more pleasure in watching the sun sink into the sea than in waiting for the curtain to rise in the Hippodrome. There is the special and extensive difficulty of lovers who, because they are in love, and therefore a little daft, prefer the song of the waves even when a prima donna is lifting the roof of the Pavilion. For those a great seaside impresario invented the Beauty Show, with its weeks of titillant expectation, its hot-pressed candidature, its night of rapturous awards and rejections by guffaw. It was a stroke of genius—nothing less—to counter the beauty of the cosmos with that of cosmetics.

The tale, of course, is not half told. The pageant, the carnival, the motor-track, and the aerodrome now attract and absorb tens of thousands of sightseers who are pumped out of the great cities by the vast machinery of advertisement. The evolution of the seaside is nearly complete, for the survival of its unfit element cannot last much longer. The Amusement Committees will see to its going, inspired by the Apocalyptic vision of a new heaven (paradise in the advertisements) when there shall be "no more sea." For my part, I had intended to wait for the full revelation. I remember when the presiding genius of the seaside was not the Mayor covered with confetti, but the bathing-woman waddling in the foam and remembering our names; when the rare acrobat spread his carpet in the street; when the star-fish, not the music-hall star, was our delight; when, for sensation, the cannon of England boomed from the fort on the cliff; when the stately ships went on to their haven under the hill; and to young eyes the Spirit of God moved on the face of the waters. It was not so long ago, and, though it may seem odd, I regret the immense change.

[*July* 29, 1910.]

ABBEYANA

MONDAY is the free day at Westminster Abbey, and passing that way last Monday afternoon I viewed from the top of a motor-bus the wonderful immemorial crowd round the north door, delaying and disappearing like bees. Could Charles Lamb return to London, could Dr. Johnson, could Addison, could Pepys, could Shakespeare himself—each would recognise that slow crowd as part of his own London. It is impossible to suppose that Shakespeare did not visit the Abbey. He may have stood among the poets who flung their quills on Spenser's coffin; it has been finely exclaimed by Stanley: "What a funeral was that at which Beaumont, Fletcher, Jonson, and, in all probability, Shakespeare attended!—what a grave in which the pen of Shakespeare may be mouldering away!" But, apart from any such occasion, who doubts that he wandered there among the tombs of the kings whose dead hearts he searched, and gazed long at the great portrait of his own Richard the Second, in sentiment the most kingly, in action the weakest of kings?

However, it was not to meditate on kings and poets that I slipped off my motor-bus, and followed a big party of Germans into the transept. There are small things in the Abbey, as well as great, and one makes a season for each. I thought I would take a true Cockney stroll round the church: see the stuffed Parrot, look for the join in Camden's nose, pick out the Islip rebuses, and pay my respects to the lady who did *not* die of a pricked finger. In the old days there were a dozen such sights in the Abbey for which the crowd had a crowd's appetite. One would not wish them back. Some were unworthy of the Abbey and the gazers. But they have now an historical interest of a sort: they do help us to see this throng of Abbey sightseers as the vanguard of an immemorial procession. One of the most famous of these attractions, and certainly the least wholesome, was the corpse of Henry V's Queen Catherine of Valois. In her widowhood the Queen began her unfortunate connection with Owen Tudor, a gentleman of the Court. A great scandal rose, Owen Tudor was imprisoned, and Catherine returned to Bermondsey Abbey, where she died in 1437.

She was buried in the Lady Chapel of Westminster Abbey. But the Lady Chapel was doomed. Henry VII was to pull it down to make room for his own magnificent and penitential annexe. When this was done Katharine's ruinous coffin was transferred to the side of her husband's tomb, and there, incredible though it may seem, it remained unburied, for nearly 200 years. The Queen's mummified remains were visible, and were the cynosure of Cockney eyes. The sight took its place for generations, in what may be called the servant-gal element in the Abbey spectacle. To-day it is an unthinkable desecration. But Londoners do not seem to have been shocked. The remains may have been shown, as they were to Pepys, by "particular favour," but they were shown freely enough. And Pepys—that servant-gal of genius—complacently writes in his diary: "I had the upper part of her body in my hands, and I did kiss her mouth, reflecting upon it that I did kiss a queene, and that this was my birthday, thirty-six years old, that I did kiss a queene." Such a state of things required explanation, and the legend grew that all was by the Queen's desire; that thus, after death, she had wished to do penance for her disobedience to her husband "for being delivered of her son, Henry VI, at Windsor, the place which he forbade." In 1778 an order was given for the re-interment of the Queen's remains, but it was not obeyed and Hutton, the Birmingham topographer, saw them seven years later. They were at last buried under the Villiers monument in the chapel of St. Nicholas. Finally, Queen Victoria

ordered the coffin to be re-interred in the chantry of Henry
V, where it now rests.

Then there was "the lady who died by pricking her
finger." Here we see an Abbey myth in the making.
Lady Elizabeth Russell was "a complete child of Westminster"—Stanley's phrase. She was born within the precincts, and she was christened in the Abbey before a
congregation which included the great Earl of Leicester
and Sir Philip Sidney. At twenty-one she died of con-
sumption, and was buried in a sculptured tomb in the
south ambulatory. Here the young lady is seen "reposing
herself in a curious wrought osier chair," and pointing to a
skull at her feet. The monument excited sympathy, and
servant-galism brought its fancies to the theme. The
crowd invented, and believed, the story that the lady's
pointing finger had been pricked by a needle, that she had
fallen asleep before staunching the infinitesimal wound, and
had bled to death! This story must have been held very
precious. Puritan prejudice soon added to it the suggestion
that the young lady had so far forgotten her duty as to
engage in sewing on a Sunday, and that this judgment had
fallen on her sin. When Sir Roger de Coverley visited the
Abbey he was led, as a matter of course, to "the Figure
which represents that Martyr to good Housewifery, who
died by the prick of a needle. Upon an Interpreter's
telling us that she was a Maid of Honour to Queen Elizabeth the Knight was very inquisitive into her Name and
Family; and after having regarded her Finger for some
time, I wonder, says he, that Sir Richard Barker has said
nothing of her in his Chronicle." In like manner Goldsmith's Chinaman was entertained with the sad recital,
but that astute gentleman from Pekin classed it promptly
among a "hundred lies" told him by his guide, and esteemed
it no more than the statement that the stone under the
Coronation chair had been Jacob's pillow.

The Abbey Poll-Parrot may still be seen.   It stands on its perch as gravely now as it did under Queen Anne.   Esme Lennox, the beautiful Duchess of Richmond, died on October 22nd, 1702, and her parrot which had been her companion for forty years, died a few days later.   Her Grace directed that her effigy in wax, clothed in the dress she wore at the coronation of Queen Anne, should be placed, as the custom then was, beside her tomb.   It is now one of the "Ragged Regiment" in the room above Abbot Islip's Chapel.   She had left annuities for her cats, as Pope tells us in his third Moral Epistle, and some sympathetic person had the idea of allowing her dead stuffed parrot to bear her company in the Abbey gloom. The lady's effigy and the bird are now safe in their glazed cupboard.

Visitors to this Chapel may notice on its screen, and in various other parts, two sculptured rebuses of Abbot Islip's name.   A boy is seen slipping from a tree (I slip); an eye is visible among slips of foliage (eye slip).   The ancients liked to button-hole posterity.

I am sorry to report that William Camden's nose is again in danger.   To my anxious eyes it cannot survive this century.   The great antiquary died in 1623, and was decently buried in the south transept opposite Poets' Corner, where his long-suffering mural tablet and bust may be seen.   Twenty-three years later the Cavaliers broke into the Abbey after the burial of Robert Devereux, Earl of Essex, the Parliamentary general, to deface his "hearse," and incidentally they "used the like uncivil deportment toward the effigies of old learned Camden—cut in pieces the book held in his hand, broke off his nose, and otherwise defaced his visiognomy."   This account is adopted by Dean Stanley in his *Memorials* of the Abbey, but another and more romantic story is told by Dr. Thomas Smith in his *Camdeni Vita*.   I find it quoted in a long footnote to Sir John Hawkins's *Life of Dr. Johnson*—a book in which one may encounter anything. This connects the outrage with the famous episode of Sir Walter Raleigh and Elizabeth Throgmorton. The story is that the mutilation was done by a young man, a relation of this lady, who was exasperated by Camden's narrative in his *Annals* of Raleigh's intrigue and subsequent marriage with the fair Devonshire girl, who was one of Queen Elizabeth's Maids of Honour. The Queen punished the peccant lovers severely: both were imprisoned in the Tower. Camden's own punishment lasted more than a century, but in 1780 the University of Oxford gave him the nose which time now gently tweaks.

[*July* 18, 1913.]

A WALK THROUGH EVERYMAN'S LONDON

WHO forgets, and who recovers, his first vision of the Abbey towers, grey above the trees, moored as it were in the sea of time, and bathed in the aura of a race? My own is enhanced in recollection by a boyish adventure. It befell that for ten minutes in the dusk of a summer evening I was locked up alone among the royal tombs. I had arrived late, and in the rustic frenzy of my fifteen years. The verger, relenting from the rules, took me up the deeply shadowed nave. Unlocking the iron gates at the south of the Sacrarium he passed me into the heart of the Abbey, telling me that I might walk round to the corresponding north gates where he would meet me in ten minutes. It was magnificent, but sudden, and I was subdued when he locked the gate and walked away in the gloom. I moved uneasily round the chapels, not fearing, I think, a kingly ghost, but the faint roar of London seemed to have become an inarticulate cosmic murmur and an insufficient assurance of life in this august home of death. Consequently I was peering through the north gate long before my time. The minutes dragged. A rush of apprehension seized me; I climbed the iron gate, ran like a deer down the aisle, and darted through the door as if royal dust were indeed stirring. Bounding into the street, I was aware of my verger musing in the entrance. He said not a word—nor I.

It must have been in a calmer mood, or with stronger nerves, that Chateaubriand, locked accidentally in the Abbey, passed a whole night there. He looked around for a lair, and found it, he tells us, "near the monument of Lord Chatham at the bottom of the gallery of the Chapel of the Knights and that of Henry VII. At the entrance to the steps leading to the aisles, shut in by folding gates, a tomb fixed in the wall, and opposite a marble figure of death with a scythe, furnished me a shelter. A fold in the marble winding-sheet served me as a niche; after the example of Charles V, I habituated myself to my interment."*

It appears, then, that I entered Westminster Abbey thirty years ago under a régime that had not begun the enforcement of strict rule and the scrutiny of handbags; the old era of official insousiance had left a chink through which a country boy could be allowed to wander at his will in the mausoleum. This gives me a sense of another, an older, London—the London that changed perhaps on that Sunday afternoon in 1887, when into the whirlpool of Trafalgar Square the Grenadiers marched from St.

* It is not possible to identify the spot from Chateaubriand's description, which seems to be muddled.

I

George's Barracks with ball cartridge, and the Life Guards came pricking up Whitehall with quite a new kind of glitter. A great deal of the picturesque ruination in the Abbey to-day is due less to the attritions of Time than to such indulgence as I had received. Many who formerly came to meditate remained to carve. The Coronation Chair is covered with the initials of these disastrous folk, who often found leisure to add the date of their depredations. Some of them cut their honest names on the State Shield of Edward III. Others, bent more on relics than personal immortality, removed mosaic and jewels and brass plates, or wrenched off the minor images and ornaments from the great tombs. The shrine of Edward the Confessor is now a dull erection of stones; formerly it blazed with many golden statuettes, each decked with insignia set with rubies, onyx, and pearls. It displayed fifty-five large cameos, and where there was no such encrustation the fabric was aglow with mosaic. Hardly a handbreadth of this splendour remains. The silver head of the effigy of Henry III was stolen centuries ago. "Some Whig, I'll warrant you," suggested Sir Roger de Coverley; "you ought to lock up your kings better; they will carry off the body too if you don't take care."

*   *   *   *   *

Dean Stanley has pointed out that of the three greatest names in England's roll of intellect, Shakespeare, Bacon, and Newton, only the last is inscribed on an Abbey tomb. Shakespeare has a monument, Bacon nothing. There are no monuments to Keats, Shelley and Byron. Cowley is honoured there, but not Waller; Beaumont, but not Herrick; Denham and Drayton, but not Marlowe and Suckling. Milton's parodist, John Philips, was given a monument in the Abbey at a time when Milton's own name was considered as an impossible "pollution of its walls." Some absences have been too glaring to be endured.

Robert Burns was given a bust forty years ago; Scott a bust only seven years ago; and Coleridge's bust was unveiled by Mr. Lowell in 1885. On the other hand, Matthew Arnold is represented by a bust, though few visitors find it; here promptitude is matched by modernity, for you may study the cut of the great critic's coat and the shape of his collar and necktie. In the same dark corner which has received Arnold's bust Wordsworth is represented by a feeble and moping statue; why is not our greatest poet since Milton honoured in Poets' Corner?

Chaucer's grave was the magnet to poetic dust. His grey marble tomb, erected a century and a half after his death, is still the most beautiful and venerable object in this part of the Abbey. He had but a short journey to take from his bed to his grave, for his last days were spent in a tenement in the Abbey garden, on ground now covered by the Chapel of Henry VII. His last words, said to have been dictated on his death-bed, should always be given in connection with Chaucer's passing:

> Here is no home, here is but wilderness.
> Forth, pilgrim, forth! O beast, out of thy stall,
> Look up on high, and thank thy God of all.
> Control thy lust; and let thy spirit thee lead;
> And Truth shall thee deliver; 'tis no dread.

Spenser, Drayton, Tennyson, and Browning lie near the father of English verse. Spenser's first Latin epitaph, long superseded, contained the words:

> Hic prope Chaucerum situs est Spenserius illi
> Proximus ingenio, proximus et tumulo.

This inscription, set up by Anne Clifford, Countess of Dorset, was replaced in 1778 by an epitaph which described Spenser as "the prince of poets in his tyme." A year or two ago the crowbars fell on little King Street, where the

poet of all virtue died on a tavern bed.   From this street—
the old royal way into the Abbey precincts—he was
followed to his grave by his brother poets, who presently
threw their elegies and their quills upon his coffin.   Of
these mourners Francis Beaumont was the next to be laid
in Poets' Corner.

Drayton followed, and again an Anne Clifford was the
giver of a poet's monument.   Ben Jonson usually receives
the credit of the epitaph, but Quarles may deserve it.   It
is good to know that Ben is in the Abbey.   Poverty and
neglect darkened his latter days.   Some premonition that
he might be shut out of the noble company seems to have
haunted his mind.   There is an Abbey legend that points
to this.   It is said that one day, being rallied by the Dean
of Westminster about being buried in Poets' Corner,
Jonson remarked: "I am too poor for that, and no one
will lay out funeral charges upon me.   No, sir, 6 feet
long by 2 feet wide is too much for me; 2 feet by 2 will
do all I want."   "You shall have it," said the Dean.
Apocryphal as the story sounds, its essential truth is
supported by the fact that in 1849, when Sir Robert Watson's
grave was being made, the Clerk of the Works "saw the
two leg-bones of Jonson fixed bolt upright in the sand, as
though the body had been buried in the upright position;
and the skull came rolling down among the sand from a
position above the leg-bones, to the bottom of the newly
made grave.   There was still hair upon it, and it was of a
red colour."   Unfortunately the grave is not in Poets'
Corner, as Jonson's bust (on the same wall as the monuments
of Spenser and Milton) may lead the pilgrim to believe.
The slab with the words *O Rare Ben Jonson* cut upon
it is in the north aisle of the nave.   The stone has been
placed against the wall for its better preservation.

The coming of Dryden in 1700 was a great event in the
annals of Poets' Corner.   No poet has a simpler and nobler

monument.   Chaucer's tombstone is said to have been sawn
asunder in the making of his grave.   At first he had no
epitaph and Pope drew attention to the homelessness of
"Dryden's awful dust" in his epitaph for Rowe:

> Beneath a rude and nameless stone he lies,
> To which thy tomb shall guide inquiring eyes.

It is said to have been on this hint that Dryden's patron,
Sheffield, Duke of Buckinghamshire, erected a bust, which
was soon replaced by the present one, a masterpiece of
Scheemakers'.   Dryden is one of those poets whose
enmities needed the "reconciliations" of the Abbey.   It
is curious, nevertheless, that Shadwell's bust and Dryden's
are removed as far from each other as possible, and that
their faces are averted from each other's gaze in a way
that is rather amusing when noticed on the spot.

Next to Shadwell rests Dryden's far more dangerous
critic, Prior, who ridiculed his reign at Will's Coffee-house.
Why is Prior so little remembered as a man?   He must have
been a delightful fellow, or he could not have spent so
many evenings with Swift; the Diary to Stella is full of
Prior.   He was liker to Horace than any poet we have
bred, though he rather desired Horace's life than lived it.
The wish for the simple life needs no better expression
than he gave to it:

> Great Mother, let me once be able
> To have a garden, house, and stable,
> That I may read, and write, and plant,
> Superior to desire or want;
> And as health fails, and years increase,
> Sit down, think, and die in peace.

Addison had preceded Prior to the Abbey by two years.
He was, so to speak, born to be buried in the Abbey.   His
piety, his learning, his wit, his predilections, and his

achievements fitted and entitled him to such honour.   And
his is a classic Abbey funeral.   "On the north side of that
Chapel," says Macaulay, "in the vault of the House of
Albemarle, the coffin of Addison lies next to the coffin
of Montague.   Yet a few months, and the same mourners
passed again along the same aisle.   The same sad anthem
was again chanted.   The same vault was again opened;
and the coffin of Craggs was placed close to the coffin of
Addison."   Macaulay himself now lies close to Addison.

The funeral of Isaac Newton was less remarkable for
its pomp than for the fact that among those who gathered
round the grave was Voltaire.   To Newton was allotted
one of the two fine positions on either side of the entrance
to the Choir.   This position had been refused to various
noblemen who had applied for it.

One of the most showy of Abbey burials was Garrick's.
It cost £1,500.   There were thirty-three mourning coaches
alone, and each was drawn by six horses.   When the
extravagance of the funeral was being discussed, and the
six horses to each coach were mentioned by Mrs. Burney,
Dr. Johnson snapped out: "Madam, there were no more
six horses than six phœnixes."   But there were.   Johnson
himself rode in the nineteenth coach, and Gibbon was in the
twentieth.   At intervals men in cloaks rode on horseback,
and the coaches were attended by pages.   The coffin was
covered with crimson velvet.   All traffic was stopped for
two hours while the immense procession made its way
from Adelphi Terrace.   Many people sat on the house-
tops.   In the Abbey, Burke suggested that the statue of
Shakespeare seemed to be pointing to Garrick's open
grave.

Sheridan was buried near to Garrick and Johnson.   His
coffin was carried by dukes, earls, and a bishop.   It is no
wonder, considering the circumstances of his end, that a
French newspaper remarked that "France is the place

for a man of letters to live in, and England the place for him to die in."

It is curious that the body of Sheridan, for whom Byron had so much liking, and whose character he defended, rested in Great George Street, waiting burial in the Abbey, and that Byron's remains lay there only to be turned from the Abbey doors. Macaulay refers to this accident, and to the feelings of those who saw the long train of coaches turn slowly northwards, "leaving behind it that cemetery which had been consecrated by the dust of so many great poets, but of which the doors were closed against all that remained of Byron." Dean Stanley refused to judge harshly either Byron's claims to an Abbey burial or the convictions of those who refused it. But his own sympathies are clear. "If Byron was turned from the door, many a one as questionable as Byron has been admitted. Close above the monument of the devoted Granville Sharpe is the monument of the epicurean St. Evremond. Close behind the tablet of the blameless Wharton lies the licentious Congreve." It was on 12 July, 1824, that the strange scene was enacted. Byron had died on 19 April at Missolonghi. Twenty-one days' mourning by the Greeks had followed, and it was not until 2 May that the body was embarked, amid the firing of minute-guns, on the brig *Florida* for England. Even the news of his death did not reach London until 14 May. It is impossible to convey an idea of the impression made when the words ran through England—"Byron is dead." Men's breath was taken away to hear that this man, whose excess of life was manifested alike in his virtues and faults, in his genius and personality, had died in an endeavour to free Greece. In one of his letters Byron had protested that he would never allow his dead body to be brought home like Nelson's in a cask; and, indeed, if the spectacular element in his life had been allowed to rule the manner of his burial, he would not have been laid to his rest like a

county magnate in the heart of England.   On some lonely
Aegean isle, or on some Grecian promontory, dear to poet
and historian, Byron's obelisk would have caught the
first and last rays of the sun.

But on 1 July the ship *Florida* brought his remains to
the Downs.   It was known that an application for an
Abbey burial would be refused, and it had been decided
that Byron should be laid in the family vault at Hucknall
Torkard, a mile or two from Newstead Abbey, amid the
scenes which had been associated with his boyish passion
for Mary Chaworth.   It seems probable that his remains
were brought to Westminster by the very route over which,
with infinite vivacity of description, he had made Don
Juan enter London.

On the 12th Thomas Moore breakfasted with Samuel
Rogers.   At half-past nine they set off.   George Street,
as they saw it, has virtually disappeared in recent years.
When Moore saw the house and the crowd and the under-
taker's men, he was seized with a nervous trembling
amounting to illness.   The scene lives in his Diary.   The
procession started, Moore riding in a coach along with
four others—Rogers, Campbell, Colonel Stanhope, and a
Greek Deputy.   As they turned out of George Street he
saw a lady crying in a barouche, and said to himself: "Bless
her heart, whoever she is."   Most of the mourners left
the procession at St. Pancras turnpike, and returned to
town.   It was not until he was crossing the Park with
Rogers that Moore felt the full pathos of the day.   Here,
strangely enough, they met a soldier's funeral, and the bugles
were wailing out the air, *I'm wearin' awa' like snaw
wreaths*.   Had they continued the journey north they
would have seen much else to move their feelings.   As the
cortège wound its way up through Kentish Town it passed
a small house, from the windows of which it was watched
by the widows of Shelley and Captain Williams, whose

husbands' drowned bodies had been burned in Byron's presence on the wild beach at Leghorn. Mrs. Shelley wrote afterwards: "What should I have said to a Cassandra who, three years ago, should have prophesied that Jane and I—Williams and Shelley gone—should watch the funeral procession of Lord Byron up Highgate Hill? All changes of romance or drama lag far behind this."

*   *   *   *   *

The contiguity of the Houses of Parliament to the Abbey is one of the impressive things of London. The Abbey, Westminster Hall, St. Stephen's, and the Government offices combine to make a great group of national symbols. Their neighbourliness is, of course, a matter of development rather than design, yet less than eighty years ago there was a danger that this great national congeries would be broken up for ever.

The story is worth retelling. On the night of 16 October, 1834, a man of forty was one of an excited band of passengers on the coach from Brighton to London. Far away on the horizon a red light was pulsing wickedly, and at intervals a bright glow struck the clouds above. At last the passengers' shouts of inquiry were answered. The Houses of Parliament were on fire. In this, as in every other direction, the news had travelled fast. At Dudley it was known within three hours. To the man of forty on the Brighton coach it meant more than to most people. Charles Barry had been born under the Palace of Westminster; and now, as the sky reddened, the thought came to him that he might be chosen to rebuild it—a true presentiment.

An appalling spectacle awaited the travellers. The sky was invaded by smoke and embers, and from every suburb crowds were pouring to the bridges. Three regiments of Guards had turned out. The crowd knew that the home of British liberty, the sanctuary of civil rights, perhaps the Hall of Rufus itself—unrivalled in the world, and

dear now, if it never was before, to their hearts—were in
the greatest peril. And it had but one thought: could
Westminster Hall be saved? At the centre that hope
became determined effort. Engines were taken into the
interior, ready to pour water into Richard the Second's
oaken roof. It was a scene which men were to remember
on their death-beds. An eye-witness says that behind
the dreadful pother the grey towers of the Abbey seemed
asleep in the moonlight, unconscious of the red tinge
that played among her buttresses.

From the sublime to the ridiculous there is never more
than a step. Old Dean Ireland, aghast and dusty, was
standing with his Keeper of the Records on the roof of
the Abbey Chapter House. A gust of wind swept the
flames towards them. The Keeper, foreseeing even more
dreadful things, implored him to descend and save the
inestimable treasures of the church. But John Ireland
was not a Very Reverend Dean in an Established Church for
nothing. He knew his place, and while the sparks were
blowing over Henry the Seventh's Chapel he firmly replied
that he could not think of moving anything without
permission from the First Lord of the Treasury. Yet had
he gone to consult Lord Melbourne he would certainly
have been rewarded with an oath.

When the fire was in hand London breathed again. Hall
and Abbey stood untouched amid the acres of smoking ruins.
The cause of this unparalleled disaster is one of the jests of
history, and it was never told with more humour than by
Charles Dickens. In an after-dinner speech at Drury Lane
Theatre he said:

"Ages ago a savage mode of keeping accounts on
notched sticks was introduced into the Court of Exchequer,
and the accounts were kept much as Robinson Crusoe
kept his calendar on the desert island, on certain splints
of elmwood called *tallies*.

"In the Reign of George III an inquiry was made by some revolutionary spirit whether—pens, ink, and paper, slates and pencils, being in existence—this obstinate adherence to an obsolete custom ought to be continued, and whether a change ought not to be effected. All the red tape in the country grew redder at the bare mention of this bold and original conception, and it took till 1826 to get these sticks abolished. In 1834 it was found that there was a considerable accumulation of them; and the question then arose—what was to be done with such worn-out, rotten old bits of wood? It came to pass that they were burnt in a stove in the House of Lords. The stove, overgorged with these preposterous sticks, set fire to the panelling; the panelling set fire to the House of Lords; the House of Lords set fire to the House of Commons; the two houses were reduced to ashes; architects were called in to build others; and we are now in the second million of the cost thereof; the national pig is not nearly over the stile yet; and the little old woman, Britannia, hasn't got home to-night."

The old Palace of Westminster was all but destroyed. St. Stephen's Chapel, where the House of Commons had sat for centuries, was reduced to a few blackened walls. It had been set apart during the reign of Edward VI for the use of the House of Commons, and the last day on which the House sat there was 25 September, 1834. On its site has arisen the fine vestibule named St. Stephen's Hall, the walls of which exactly correspond with those of the old Chapel. The spot which the Speaker's Chair occupied is carefully marked, and also the place where stood the table from which Cromwell removed the mace, and on which Pitt and Burke and Fox laid their papers. Below the floor the beautiful Crypt Chapel still remains as one of the few relics of the old Palace. Privileged babies are baptized at its font, and once in an age a Lord Chancellor is married there.

When the last fire-engine had trotted home, when King William and Queen Adelaide had driven down in two closed carriages to inspect the débris, and when the Privy Council had solemnly reported that somebody had done something improper, the question of immediate accommodation for Parliament presented itself. At a cost of £30,000 the Lords were sent into the Painted Chamber, the Commons into the damaged House of Lords. The results were different: the Lords were uncomfortable, and decided that Barry was a slow architect; the Commons liked their quarters so well that they were in no hurry to move into Barry's new chamber when it was ready.

Ninety-seven architects had been tempted by the premiums and the opportunity. It was understood that a splendid building, in the Elizabethan or Gothic styles, would be sanctioned. Barry's plan, No. 64, was awarded the first premium. He had spent the available time (six months) in the hardest labour, never allowing himself more than five hours' sleep, and he had made a tour of the town halls of Belgium before working out his design. His son tells us that his first plan was sketched on the back of a letter in a friend's house, and that this was the germ of all that followed. The plan he submitted was curtailed, and altered in the execution beyond belief, yet out of the welter of schemes and counter-schemes there emerged the perpendicular Gothic conception which the world applauds to-day.

The low site chosen for the building was an obstacle to magnificent effect, all the more so because old Westminster Bridge had a much higher pitch and a taller parapet than its successor. A proposal was made to elevate the new Palace on a great terrace, like that of Somerset House, but it was seen that this would woefully dwarf Westminster Hall and the Abbey. There was also an idea of removing Parliament to the Green Park or to Trafalgar Square, but the associations of history forbade. In a recent discussion at the Architectural Association it was mentioned that the Duke of Wellington favoured the river-edge site on the characteristic ground that the Houses of Parliament ought not to be accessible on all sides to a mob!

The national region of London, as it may be called, is but "irregularly great," but it homes itself about the Abbey in large and impressive groupings and areas. Within a few minutes one may see, besides the great Westminster buildings, the long line of Government offices, the Banqueting Hall of the Stuarts, the Horse Guards and its Parade, the old Admiralty, the Nelson Monument, old St. James's, the Mall, and the Palace. Parliament Street and Whitehall are resonant with great names and happenings. Milton lodged in Scotland Yard while Latin secretary to Cromwell, and Andrew Marvell succeeded to his office and residence.

Something of the old Cromwellian air of Whitehall lingers in Whitehall Court, behind the Banqueting House of unhappy memory. Here are little forecourt gardens and green painted window-boxes, and pigeons ambling about in the sunshine, and one hears the golden notes of Big Ben. The house in which Sir Robert Peel died looks down on the quiet precinct.

Unless custom has staled the experience one does not stand on the Horse Guards' Parade unmoved. Though it may be empty as the Sahara or flecked with nothing more interesting than a Cabinet Minister and a water-cart the spirit is stirred. The bugles of empire seem to be faintly blowing across this fine level, round which the buildings of bleached stone or mellow brick rise with significant neatness and power. Yonder is the dragon bomb which Spain gave to the Prince Regent, and away there in a corner, almost lost in its own sombreness of brick and ivy, is the eighteenth-century wall which makes snug the garden of all that messuage, No. 10 Downing Street.

The most interesting building in Whitehall is beyond question the old Admiralty, built in the reign of the first George by Ripley, and described by Walpole as "a most ugly edifice, and deservedly veiled by Mr. Adams's handsome screen." In the room to the left of the entrance door lay in state the body of Nelson. The Marconi apparatus on the roof is perhaps the most fascinating object in London, for through that delicate web of wires England speaks to her war captains around her coasts and for many hundreds of miles to sea. These Marconi masts have taken the place, on the same roof, of ordinary telegraph wires, which had superseded the hand-worked semaphore by which in Nelson's day a message was sent to the next station in St. George's Fields, and thence from point to point until from the cliffs it sped to the quarter-deck. The rapidity with which messages could be sent down from the Admiralty to Portsmouth through that old chain of semaphore signals was remarkable, and some of the stories of quick communication almost pass belief. From the Admiralty roof a message was transmitted through Chelsea, Putney, Kingston, and thence by Cooper's Hill, Chately Hill, and five other hills to Compton Down, Portsdown Hill, and Southsea Beach, until, finally it was received on a tower in High Street, Portsmouth. It is said that a message could be thus sent from Whitehall to Portsmouth in less than a minute.

*   *   *   *   *

It was once intended that Cleopatra's Needle should be erected at the foot of Waterloo Place on the spot where the Crimea monument stands. It may be remembered that when those weighty critics of "Life in London," the Hon. Tom Dashall and Squire Tallo-ho, were admiring the features of Waterloo Place, then known as Regent's Place, the aesthetic squire remarked that there was a vacuum on this spot. His friend agreed, but informed him that the column known as Cleopatra's Needle was "destined to raise its lofty summit in Regent's Place." This idea remained in the air until the fifties, the Needle on its part remaining in the sands of Alexandria, where Thackeray saw it "desecrated by all sorts of abominations." In the interval, the disappointed shareholders of Waterloo Bridge asked in vain to have the Needle placed on the Central arch of the bridge as an attraction to passengers.

The story of Carlton House is the story of a whole period, and it is in many books. But one rather unfamiliar record comes to mind. Here the American Minister of the Waterloo period, Mr. Rush, saw a very remarkable crowd just after the battle—a number of wounded British officers of high distinction basking in the smiles of the Regent. He describes the unusual scene as follows:

There were from forty to fifty generals: perhaps as many admirals, with throngs of officers of rank inferior. I remarked upon the number of wounded. Who is that, I asked, pallid but with a countenance so animated? 'That's General Walker,' I was told, 'he was pierced with bayonets, leading on the assault as Badajos.' And he, close by, tall but limping? 'Colonel Ponsonby; he was left for dead at Waterloo; the cavalry it was thought had trampled upon him.' Then came one of like port, but deprived of a leg, slowly moving; and the whisper went: 'That's Lord Anglesea.' A fourth had been wounded at Seringapatam; a fifth at Talavera; some had suffered in Egypt, some in America. There were those who had received scars on the deck with Nelson; others who had carried them from the days of Howe. One, yes, one had fought at Saratoga. It was so that my inquiries were answered. Each 'did his duty:' this was the favourite praise bestowed. The great number of wounded was accounted for by recollecting that little more than two years had elapsed since the armies and fleets of Britain had been liberated from wars of extraordinary fierceness and duration in all parts of the globe. For, so it is, other nations chiefly fight on or near their own territory; the English everywhere.

The only great and deliberate scheme for building a royal palace in London is that of which Inigo Jones's Banqueting Hall is the monument and the fragment. The story of Buckingham Palace is but serio-comic. It is a curious coincidence that George V's London home stands upon ground that is associated with a "Wake up, England!" gospel preached (somewhat fantastically) by James I. In 1609 James addressed a circular to the Sheriffs, Deputy-Lieutenants, and others, in which he expressed his royal anxiety "to wean his people from idleness and the enormities thereof." He had an idea for making his subjects busy and prosperous, and a very curious idea it was: to plant England with mulberry trees and establish a native silk industry. Ten thousand mulberry-saplings were to be sent to each county, and the Sheriffs and Deputy-Lieutenants were to see to the rest. James himself took four acres from St. James's Park, walled them in, and planted with mulberry-trees the ground in which Buckingham Palace stands. Mulberry planting became the fashion. It is said that one of those who fell in with it was William Shakespeare, who planted a mulberry tree in his garden at Stratford-on-Avon, where it flourished until the middle of the eighteenth century, when it was cut down by Parson Gastrill, to his everlasting local shame. The home silk industry inaugurated by James I did not flourish. In our time, nevertheless, on the spot where His Majesty's silkworms perished, a Queen has in our day ordered her Coronation robes to be made of home-spun silk.

The mulberry garden became a popular resort, and the Restoration plays teem with references to its paths and pleasures—both shady. On 10 May, 1654, Evelyn wrote in his diary: "My Lady Gerard treated us at Mulberry Garden, now the only place of refreshment for persons of the best quality to be exceedingly cheated at." Evelyn explains that since Cromwell had shut up the Spring Gardens the pleasure-seekers had moved to the other end of the Mall. Rather more than fifty years later, when old Buckingham House was built on the spot, Dr. King wrote in his *Art of Cookery* of this "princely palace" that had displaced the forlorn mulberries. Buckingham House was built for John Sheffield, Marquis of Normandy and Duke of Buckinghamshire. It was a handsome house, and the Duke was proud of his view of London seen from his flat, statue-crowned roof, and of his retired garden with its "wilderness full of blackbirds and nightingales." There were "waterworks" and Latin mottoes, and there was the gleam of the London sunshine on the "canal in the Park."

It fell out that a Prince and Princess of Wales (afterwards George II and Queen Caroline) wanted a London house, and envied Naboth his vineyard. Naboth was dead, but his widow, the Duchess, was willing to treat. Her notions were severely businesslike, and the exact terms of her offer, which have come down to us, indicate that her Grace of Buckinghamshire had the makings of an estate-agent. She wrote: "If Their Royal Highnesses will have everything stand as it does, furniture and pictures, I will have £3,000 per annum; both run hazard of being spoiled, and the last, to be sure, will all to be new bought when my son is of age. The quantity the rooms take cannot be well furnished under £10,000; but if Their Highnesses will permit the pictures all to be removed, and buy the furniture as it will be valued by different people, the house shall go at £2,000. . . . If the Prince or Princess prefer much the buying outright, it will not be parted with under £60,000, as it now stands, and all His Majesty's revenue cannot purchase a place so fit for them, nor for a less sum."

The Hanoverians were poor, and business did not result. The Duchess continued to live in her paradise at the head of the Mall, swelling with pride to remember that she was the illegitimate daughter of James II (a doubtful claim) and therefore the granddaughter of Charles I, whose martyrdom she celebrated every year in her great drawing-room, seated in a chair of state, and "surrounded by her women, all in black and dismal-looking as herself." She had a great mind to be buried at St. Germains, with her father, but thought better of it, and decided to lie with her husband in Westminster Abbey. She came as near to attending her own funeral as mortal can, for she planned its ceremonial and insisted on having the canopy brought to her bedside, "even though all the tassels are not finished."

The mansion which George II had refused at £60,000 was picked up by George III in 1762 for less than half that sum, and was settled on Queen Charlotte in place of old Somerset House, which being ruinous was about to disappear in favour of the great Civil Service palace we now know. And thus it was that Royalty came to Buckingham House.

In her Journal, under the year 1792, Fanny Burney gives a brief description of Buckingham House when "Farmer George" and his family were thoroughly settled there. Alighting at the porter's lodge, she was charmed to be in time to see the King, with his three sons, the Prince of Wales, Duke of York, and Duke of Clarence, standing there after just alighting from their horses, when the people pressed against the iron railings. "It was a pleasant and goodly sight, and I rejoiced in such a detention." She met the Princess Elizabeth in a corridor, and was presently paying her respects to the Queen, who was in her State drawing-room, her head just attired for the assembly, "but her Court dress, as usual, remaining to be put on at St. James's."

Buckingham Palace, as we see it, was built from the designs of the all-building Nash, and large alterations were made for Queen Victoria at her Accession. The insufficiently handsome east front, at last to be renewed, was then built to close in the quadrangle. Many Londoners have forgotten that the Marble Arch, copied by Nash, with modifications, from the Arch of Constantine at Rome, first stood in front of the chief entrance to Buckingham Palace. It is on record that the archway, as first designed, was found to be too small to admit the royal coach; but the mistake was remedied in time. The Marble Arch was to have been surmounted by a colossal bronze group emblematic of Victory, but this was abandoned in favour of an equestrian statue of George IV. The statue was executed by Chantrey at a cost of 9,000 guineas; but it never reached the Marble Arch, and is now in Trafalgar Square.

The alterations at Hyde Park Corner within living memory have affected the triumphal arch at the head of Constitution Hill. Formerly consecrated to War and Wellington, it is now decorated by a symbol of Peace. The arch first stood opposite the Hyde Park entrance. In 1846 it was surmounted by the most conspicuous and ugly equestrian statue ever seen in London, that of the Duke. London had warning of the æsthetic error it was about to commit, for in 1838 trial was made of the statue with a wooden figure of it, and of this erection it was remarked: "Whoever has stuck up this scenic effigy deserves thanks: it demonstrates two things—that the position is a good one, and that a bad statue placed there would be an intolerable eyesore." Nevertheless the bronze statue by Wyatt was erected, and, with all its faults, was loved. Many people bitterly deplored its removal to Aldershot. A few years ago Mr. William Royle told the readers of *Notes and Queries* that he was standing on the top of the Triumphal Arch at Hyde Park Corner when the monument was lowered from it to be removed to Aldershot. The Triumphal Arch then stood immediately opposite Decimus Burton's entrance screen to Hyde Park. The architectural effect produced when the two great portals stood opposite each other may be seen in a picture in the *Illustrated London News* of 30 June, 1860, in which a regiment of Volunteers is marching through both gateways.

Few Londoners, perhaps, remembered that the removal of this statue was mooted even before its erection was completed. This was a sore point with the Duke, who, in 1846, in his room at Apsley House, was looking alternately on the scaffolding of his rising effigy and the newspaper protests against its situation. Wyatt's colossal work had just been hoisted after the interior of the horse had been used as a dining-room by a dozen of the sculptor's congratulatory friends. John Wilson Croker said: "As soon as it was there, everybody but the great Duke seems to have wished it down again." His "everybody" included Queen Victoria and Prince Albert. The agitation was galling to the Duke, whose feelings can be gauged from these sentences in a letter to Croker: "They must be idiots to suppose that it is possible that a man who is working day and night without any object in view, excepting public benefit, will not be sensible for a disgrace inflicted upon him by the Sovereign and Government whom he is serving. The ridicule will be felt, if nothing else is." In the end the Duke's known wishes were respected, and the statue remained to be a mark for jesters and caricaturists down to 1884. Then the opportunity occurred, and was taken, to get rid of an "eyesore." Eyesore or not, the statue had filled the Londoner's eye, and people had liked to show their country cousins that the setting sun cast the shadow of the effigy on Apsley House.

The most famous private mansion in London is not quite what it seems. The stone of Apsley House encases the brick of the mansion which Lord Chancellor Bathurst erected in 1784, after some difficult negotiations with an old woman who defended her interest in an apple-stall erected on this spot. The old brick front is recalled by Thackeray in *Vanity Fair*: "And the carriage drove on, taking the road down to Piccadilly, where Apsley House and St. George's Hospital wore red jackets still; where there were oil-lamps; where Achilles was not born, nor the Pimlico arch raised." Where, also, the tollgate still obstructed the entry into London.

From *A Londoner's London* (Methuen), 1913.

THE HISTORIC SHUDDER

GUSTAVE FLAUBERT invented this striking and (in the way he applied it) most apt phrase. By the historic shudder he meant the sensation one gets when some event or condition of a past time is brought home to one with the vividness of present-day life. It is seldom conveyed in formal history and then only by the historian's resort to a recorded personal experience. Such records, however, crop up in all sorts of places, and notably, of course, in letters and diaries. Browsing along my bookshelves the other day, I took down a two-volume work into which I had not looked for long. But I had once read it carefully, as my old pencil marks in the margins showed. This was the Diary, Reminiscences, and Correspondence of Henry Crabb Robinson, Barrister-at-Law,

F.S.A. Some of my readers may barely recall his name. But he lived all through the age of Byron, Lamb, Hazlitt, Leigh Hunt, Wordsworth, and countless other great writers and otherwise notable men during a life which fell short of a century by only a few years. I noted that he was born in 1775, when Dr. Johnson had still eight years to live, and that he died when I was nearly three years old. This means that if, as a boy, Henry Crabb Robinson had been patted on the head by Dr. Johnson he might conceivably have patted me on the head in my infancy. This marvel, for I deem it such, is due to the fact that H. C. R. lived into his ninety-third year, yet died nearly thirty years older than I am now. Such actual or possible links have always interested me. His own memories go back to his third or fourth year. He remembered being frightened by the report of a gun during the illuminations, at Bury St. Edmunds, on February 15th, 1779, in honour of Admiral Keppel, whose portrait Sir Joshua Reynolds had perhaps not yet painted. He recollected hearing a discussion between someone and his mother whether the departed would be recognisable in the next world, and saying: "I shall know my grandmamma in heaven by the green ribbon round her cap." So the fact that Mrs. Crabb, who may well have been born before Queen Anne came to the throne, was thus adorned is kept alive.

At the age of six H. C. R. went to a school kept by a Mr. Blomfield, who became the grandfather of a famous Bishop of London. Of this small school he relates:—

One really interesting occurrence I recollect which I have often thought of as significant. There used to be given to the boy who was at the head of his class a box and ring, and he had a present if he could keep it a certain number of days. On one occasion I lost it, to my great sorrow, and, as I thought, very unjustly;

therefore next day I went boldly to young Blomfield, who was an usher under his father, and with a book in my hand, and with a consciousness of injured innocence, said, "Sir, you turned me down for spelling the word ———— so, but I was right after all. There, see! I was right." Mr. Blomfield smiled, patted me on the head, and said: "Well, Henry, as you read it in a printed book you are not to blame, but that's printed wrong." I was quite confounded. I believed as firmly in the infallibility of print as any good Catholic can in the infallibility of his Church. I knew that naughty boys would tell stories, but how a book could contain a falsehood was quite incomprehensible.

This is "really interesting" still, because the notion that a statement or opinion seen "in print" must be right is still as widespread as it is dangerous. To be sure there is a measure of probability that a statement which has reached print is correct because it has had to pass under other eyes than its author's. But there is no certainty or magic in print itself which can be trusted.

Another of Crabb Robinson's early memories—it seems in the light of his death so late as 1867 hardly credible—is that he was an intelligent listener to John Wesley. It is clear to me now, however, that many old Wesleyans must be alive between whom and the founder of their great Church a single life is the personal link. H. C. R. writes:—

It was, I believe, in October, 1790, and not long before his death, that I heard John Wesley in the great round Meeting-house at Colchester. He stood in a wide pulpit, and on each side of him stood a minister, and the two held him up, having their hands under his armpits. His feeble voice was barely audible. But his reverend countenance, especially his long white locks, formed a picture never to be forgotten. There was a vast crowd

of lovers and admirers.   It was for the most part pantomime, but the pantomime went to the heart.   Of the
kind I never saw anything comparable to it in after life.
This son of a Bury St. Edmunds tanner grew up to be a
lawyer, a traveller, a man of the world, a journalist, a mighty
talker and listener in good company, and a born diarist.
It is the diarist we know to-day.   He left behind him
thirty-five MS. volumes of Journals, thirty volumes of
journals of travel, thirty-two volumes of letters written
and received, four volumes of "reminiscences," and
one volume of "anecdotes."   All these are preserved
in Dr. Williams's Library in Gordon Square, Bloomsbury, and although, I believe, they have at last been
thoroughly explored, there is much left for future publication.   The two thick octavo volumes which Thomas
Sadler edited and published in the 'seventies contain, however, an excellent selection of matter.   Editors and biographers of Lamb, Hazlitt, Coleridge, and Wordsworth
cannot dispense with Crabb Robinson's material.   Thus
Lamb's account of Coleridge's conversation, in his essays,
was anticipated by H. C. R., who wrote to a friend in 1810:—

Coleridge kept me on the stretch of attention and
admiration from half-past three till twelve o'clock.   On
politics, metaphysics, and poetry, more especially on the
Regency, Kant, and Shakespeare, he was astonishingly
eloquent.   But I cannot help remarking that although
he practises all sorts of delightful tricks, and shows
admirable skill in riding his hobby, yet he may be easily
unsaddled.   I was surprised to find how one may obtain
from him concessions which lead to gross inconsistencies.
Though an incomparable declaimer and speech-maker,
he has neither the readiness nor the acuteness required
by a colloquial disputant; so that, with a sense of inferiority
which makes me feel humble in his presence, I do not
feel in the least afraid of him.   Rough said yesterday,

that he is sure Coleridge would never have succeeded at the Bar even as a speaker.

This I wrote when I knew little of him; I used afterwards to compare him as a disputant to a serpent— easy to kill, if you assume the offensive, but if you let him attack, his bite is mortal. Some years after this, when I saw Madame de Staël in London, I asked her what she thought of him: she replied: "He is very great in monologue, but he has no idea of dialogue." This I repeated, and it appeared in the *Quarterly Review*. It is proof of H. C. R.'s personal importance that Lamb, Coleridge, and Wordsworth were his diligent correspondents.

Still, Robinson's wonderful diary is not concerned wholly with men and talk. His notes on places are often of great value. In February, 1818, he visits the new Regent's Park, for the first time—when its trees were but saplings and when it adjoined open country. From it he could look north to the Highgate and Hampstead hills. "I really think," he says, in the enthusiasm of the moment, that "this enclosure with the new street [Regent Street] leading to it from Carlton House [long swept away] will give a sort of glory to the Regent's government, which will be more felt by remote posterity than the victories of Trafalgar and Waterloo, glorious as these are." His prediction requires some dilution; Regent's Park remains a glory in itself, but the Regent is remembered as George the Fourth! Just a hundred and ten years ago he rode into London by Hounslow and was told by an old man on the box of the coach that when he was a boy this road was literally lined with gibbets from which hung in chains "the carcases of malefactors blackening in the sun." Just as vivid and queer in its simplicity is his account, under June, 1833, of his sensations in his first railway journey. He left Liverpool apparently for Manchester:—

On setting off there is a slight jolt, arising from the chain catching each carriage, but, once in motion, we proceeded as smoothly as possible. For a minute or two the pace is gentle, and is constantly varying. The machine produces little smoke or steam. First in order is the tall chimney; then the boiler, a barrel-like vessel; then an oblong reservoir of water; then a vehicle for coals; and then comes, of a length infinitely extendible, the train of carriages. If all the seats had been filled, our train would have carried about 150 passengers; but a gentleman assured me at Chester that he went with a thousand persons to Newton fair. There must have been two engines then. . . . I should have observed before that the most remarkable movements of the journey are those in which trains pass one another. The rapidity is such that there is no recognizing the features of a traveller. On several occasions, the noise of the passing engine was like the whizzing of a rocket. Guards are stationed in the road, holding flags, to give notice to the drivers when to stop. Near Newton, I noticed an inscription recording the memorable death of Huskisson.

Strange reading: the historic shudder! Henry Crabb Robinson remained strong and clear-headed to the last. He was eighty when one day he turned on Professor De Morgan, who wanted to help him on with his overcoat, and said: "I look upon every man who offers to help me with my coat as a deadly enemy." It was one of his conversational tricks to say what he meant in a joking, exaggerated way, and he once said: "I have the vanity to think I know how to do this . . . it is one of the secrets of conversational tact." He was quite right.

[*December* 14, 1929.]

JUST A COUNTRY WALK

A T a time when road traffic is discussed in terms of
life and death it is curious to read that there is likely
to be a great revival of walking this summer, and that
while the horse has been driven from the highway Shanks's
mare is eager to leave her stable. Walking is to be
organised. I read of parties that are to be made up, of
hostels for men and women trampers, of waterproof
ordnance maps, and of tents that can be carried in the
pocket. The prospect does not excite me particularly,
because I have always been a walker, and I never walk with
any other guidance, companionship, or objective than my
own. I do not wish to walk and talk at the same time,
and I care little for plans and programmes. Recently
Viscount Grey told multitudinous "listeners-in" that when
he visits Kew Gardens he studies carefully the notice board
at the gates, which informs the public what special attractions they may find by diligent search. Quoting him,
that very bright writer, "Lorna" of the *British Weekly*, says:
"My own practice, I am afraid, is to read the notices—
and ignore them." She obeyed only so far as to go to the
Palm House and look at bananas hanging in clusters.
Well, you can see bananas hanging, in much the same
way, in the fruit shops. And "Lorna" then "wandered
to the river edge, where hardly a soul was in sight." In
walking I like to follow my nose, forget any purpose I
had, and put up no match against time. I always liked a
story told of W. R. Greg, the author of *Enigmas of Life*.
He went out with a highly organised party of tourists to
Egypt, and there came the important time when they took
a steamer up the Nile to visit the great Temple of Philæ.
It was a long river voyage, and at some intermediate place
of call most of the party went ashore for an hour or two.

When the time came to re-embark, Greg was found lying on his back on a desert ridge gazing up into the speckless blue sky.   To the great concern of his friends he intimated that he was very happy where he was and did not think that he very much wanted to see the Temple of Philæ.   So he remained, and basked, and thought his own thoughts until the boat returned and picked him up; and he never saw the great Temple of Philæ.   On the whole I love to see the world without its "sights."   I can make an intimate friend of any common country road, but I want light and distance and air like wine, and these are to be had almost anywhere.   The "lang drierch road" to nowhere in particular gives me all I really want.

There is a six-mile stretch of road partly in but mostly out of sight of the sea that comes to mind.   I will not give it locality or name, for that is outside my purpose. There is little on that road to draw tourist or tripper, little, perhaps, that you envy me.   There are two fine old parish churches, two sets of almshouses, a few boarding-schools, several farms with their huddle of roofs, stacks, barns, and strawyards and their populous hen-coops, styes, and cow-byres.   And there are great expanses of crop-fields where I love to watch growing wheat, barley, and oats, broccoli, and turnips.   Many people, I am sure, would find this road dullness itself.   Yet some of the greatest landscape art has been inspired by such scenes.   Rembrandt had only the flat plains of Holland and its sluggish canals and wind-mills to look at, but he made etchings and drawings of them that are now almost priceless.   A thatched hut, a barn, and a mud-track under a vast sky gave him enough. Constable was satisfied with tame Essex scenery, but he drenched it in the clear beauty of sun and rain.   The secret of enjoying such scenes is to know them in all their seasonal moods, and to let these play upon the mind.   Nothing is too small for notice.   Wordsworth did not really depend on his glorious lake country for inspiration. He would have found it anywhere. Everyday Nature teaches one so much about everyday life.

Above my winding, dipping, and rising road, and all these ordinary farm fields, rises the square flint tower of a village church, seen and lost, near or distant. The arches of its nave are Norman. It is said that the tower was badly shaken by an earthquake in the reign of Elizabeth, but it has been restored in my own lifetime. There are some fifteenth and sixteenth century brasses in the interior, and a tomb to a mighty village Samson who is said to have been able to lift a weight of 160 stone and to pull against the strongest horse. You may read his epitaph:—

> Herculean Hero! Fam'd for Strength
> At last Lies here his Breadth & Length.
>
> See How the Mighty Man is Fall'n!
> To Death yᵉ Strong and Weak are all one.
>
> And the Same Judgment doth Befall,
> Goliath Great, as David Small.

All the human history of the old village can be read, without book, in its churchyard, which has become a bird sanctuary. There lies a distinguished friend of mine who, after long Civil Service career in the East, spent his last years in this village among his books. He was one of the last men to bear the now obsolete rank of "Colonel" in the Civil Service of India. Now he sleeps among the sleepers. When I passed by his grave the other day in the golden afternoon I could not but remember and repeat Byron's lines, about the finest he ever wrote:—

> . . . when I stood beneath the fresh green tree
> Which, living, waves where thou didst cease to live,
> And saw around me the wide field revive

With fruits and fertile promise, and the Spring
Come forth her work of gladness to contrive,
With all her reckless birds upon the wing,
I turned from all she brought to those she could not bring.

A local guide-book reminds me that from the churchyard there is a field path all the way to the town, "which pedestrians will find much pleasanter than the road." Well, I am Philistine enough to prefer the road, on which you pass the farms and meet the life of the country-side. The cottages, too, are there and the school-children. Lowly life in the country is delightful to watch and a labourer's "Good night" is heart-warming in the dusk.

Houses on the road-side always interest me. I like to estimate their ages by their architecture and by such trifles as garden railings. I pass a big flint-built barn into the front of which the date 1802 has been worked. I stop to read the time on the clock of a fine range of brick-built almshouses founded in 1709 under the will of a Quaker who loved his fellow-men, and whom the dedicatory tablet says:—

> In Much Weakness
> The God of Might did bless
> With Increase of Store
> Not to maintain Pride or Idleness
> But to relieve the Poor
> Such Industrius Poor
> As truly fear the Lord.

A little foot-weary, I come to an old inn called *The First and Last*. Its parlour fire is bright and its beer good. On a wall hangs a really curious document, a reproduction of the oldest Licensing Laws in the World. While a game of darts is being played in the next room, I study this document. Its inscriptions in cuneiform characters were found in Babylon on a black diorite slab, eight feet high, by a French Government expedition. These licensing laws are 4,150 years old and were enacted by Khammabari, King of Babylon, who reigned about 2250 years B.C.   Their proclamation was translated by Mr. St. Chad Boscawen, an eminent authority on Babylon.   A cast of the original slab is in the British Museum.   The Babylonian wine-shops were kept exclusively by women, who were under strict legal control and were subject to heavy penalties for any breach of the few simple laws imposed on them.   If a wine-merchant demanded silver for her drink instead of the prescribed currency, which was corn, the authorities would call her to account and order her a ducking.   If she harboured riotous characters dangerous to the State her penalty was death.   Priestesses were forbidden to trade in drink or to enter a wine-shop under penalty of being burned alive, though otherwise they were allowed to trade and some of them grew wealthy.   If a wine-merchant had given credit for sixty quarts of beer "to quench thirst" she was entitled to fifty measures of grain when harvest began, the corn harvest being the period for settling all debts.   In the later Babylonian period deeds of partner-ship and inventories of casks, cups, plate, and stores of wine and beer were entered into legally, and many of these have been discovered.

Close to the inn rises from its large grave field the old parish church of the town, containing Norman and Saxon work and some great old Bibles.   The grave-stones are a study in old family history.   This is the only churchyard in which I have seen inscribed the name of a female child "aged 1 day."   She died on July 14th, 1829, and was christened "Frances Mary."   Half a mile away you come into all the Modernities of a popular seaside resort and to the ketches flying their vanes under the harbour light-house.   Just a country walk, but I have not wearied of it in many years.

[*April* 5, 1930.]

E. V. L.*

DEDICATING his new book to three asterisks, Mr. Lucas says that his first *Punch* editor, F. C. Burnand, said that the books which men write about themselves fall into two categories, autobiography and ought-not-to-be-ography, and that he does not know to which his own belongs. It belongs to neither. It is a wayward and most prosperous trawl of memory. If any philosophy of life is here its parts cannot be assembled, though they can be vividly seen. Incidentally, Mr. Lucas explains that his book is due to a sudden and prolonged attack of lumbago. Laid up for five weeks, he found it impossible to invent among pillows, but amusing to remember: hence . . . Well, I, too, have suffered, though not so badly, from lumbago, but it never occurred to me that it could be used to disarm criticism. Actually, I think, lumbago and literature go well together; they do so in this finely-produced volume.

I am not absolutely certain whether Lucas and I were at the great Quaker school of Ackworth together or not, whether he came to it just before or just after I left, but it was one or the other. As he was then (and presumably is still) four years my junior, I should never have seen much of him among 180 boys. Nor did he stay long. I knew that Lucas was educated like a shuttlecock, but it is only now I learn that he was at nine schools between the ages at which I was at three—six too many I should suggest. When I first really knew him he was about as far in his teens as I was out of mine. That was in 1892. We were already both in the writing way. He had put in about four years as a reporter and adventurous scribbler in Brighton, and I was concerned with Quaker publications in London. He had come to piece together his nine

* *Reading, Writing and Remembering: A Literary Record*, by E. V. Lucas. With 31 plates and 50 illustrations in the text (Methuen, 18s. net).

educations at University College. His tether, he tells us, was £200, a sum for which, I dimly remember, he found some ex-collegiate uses. This college set was a bright one; it included a budding doctor, a budding borough surveyor, and the present Statistician General of Tasmania, Mr. L. F. Giblin. Lucas drank culture at University College as a camel drinks after desert marches. He was deeply influenced and wisely advised there by that master critic, W. P. Ker, Professor of English Literature, on whose lectures he hung hungrily. Ker was the very man for him, because he added to vast literary attainments many other abilities and interests: he was a playgoer, a dancer, and a mighty country walker. As a conversational critic he talked from the shoulder. E. V. L. says:—

No one that I ever knew used so few words as W. P. or did more with them. His "Good" was worth pages of elaborate praise; his "Bad" was a death sentence . . . of his hero, Sir Walter Scott, he loved every word, even the prefaces; of Wordsworth, too. In fact, there was no excellence in all literature, from Greek to Scandinavian, that he did not relish and extol. But his condemnations were as emphatic as his praises. I shall always remember his comment when I told him that William Sharp had confided to a friend of mine that whenever he was preparing to write as Fiona Macleod he dressed himself entirely in woman's clothes. "Did he?" said W. P.—"the bitch!"

From such a teacher you might expect such a pupil. Mr. Lucas does not include an example of his master's wit, at its driest, of which he once told me. Ker was walking a country road with another scholar, much less versatile than himself, when a lithe little animal crossed their path. "Hallo, a stoat!" said Ker, to which his friend replied, sceptically, "That's not my idea of a stoat." "Maybe not," retorted Ker, "but it's God's idea of a stoat."

E. V. L. was now rapidly multiplying his own literary

L

likes and dislikes. He met a good many living poets, but the man-of-letters whom he set up as a more useful model was that amazingly fecund writer, George Augustus Sala, of the *Daily Telegraph*, and writer of the famous *olla podrida*, "Echoes of the Week," in the *Illustrated London News*—a discipleship, however, which did not last. A really fresh story about Mr. Bernard Shaw is rare, but here is Mr. Lucas's encounter with him at this formative period.

I have more reason than most people to be grateful to Bernard Shaw, for in addition to giving one the pleasure of his books and plays, he taught me to swim. We were staying in the same cottage in Cornwall and bathing every day, and he, one of the best swimmers in the world, took me in hand and made what had been so difficult before simple and safe. I followed him less easily on land, for his talk was about things which I had never analysed but took for granted, with emphasis always laid on the folly and wrongheadedness of every one else. Counsels of perfection too often. He also bewildered me, unfamiliar then with the iron laws of individualism, by saying that a short story for children which I had just written, called *The Ameliorator*, the teaching of which was that we should do things for others, was the "most immoral thing he had ever read."

Other authors to whom E. V. L. desired to play the more or less "sedulous ape" were Oliver Wendell Holmes (an excellent choice), John Burroughs, Goldsmith in *The Citizen of the World*, Augustine Birrell and Andrew Lang. But he was rapidly becoming himself.

I was Lucas's first publisher, not in name, it is true, or in any financial way, yet very much so in fact. His opportunity to write his first book, *Bernard Barton and His Friends*, came to him through me; I am not sure that he met the real publisher, my employer, at all. He says:—

It was to Whitten that the manuscript had to be

delivered. I forget the date on which I promised to deliver it, but I remember this, that I faithfully carried it just before midnight to Whitten's house, and, as I could get no response to knocks and rings, deposited it (as though it were a baby at the Foundling Hospital) on the doorstep, where it was found the next morning with the milk.

Yes, I took both in myself—gasping to think what might have happened—but when I remonstrated with E. V. for risking the entire loss of his labour he would only reply, "I am a fatalist." He was that even more than he knew, for this book, published in a small edition in 1893, put Lucas's feet on the highway of his Elian studies and led him to produce by far the best Life and Edited Works of Lamb that we possess. Another and more intimate sequel was a visit I paid to his friend, Mrs. Edward FitzGerald (formerly Lucy Barton), at her Croydon home. To meet an old lady who was not only the widow of the transfuser of Omar Khayyám, but had been, as Lucy Barton, the little girl to whom Charles Lamb wrote his album verses beginning "Little book surnamed of white," was a memorable treat.

I am glad that Mr. Lucas gives a chapter to that good old (and to both of us most helpful) London evening newspaper, the *Globe*. He was for some years on the staff, and helped to produced its witty *By the Way* column of paragraphs, "each with a joke or a sting in it," bearing on the morning's news. At that time this was the only column of its kind. He inside, and I outside, the office were eager contributors of the famous *Globe* "Turnover," a light essay which began in the last column of the front page and ended near the top of the first column in the second. For these light essays the payment was one guinea, and we were keen on guineas—so much so that Lucas put it to me one day that a good turnover ought to appear more than once, in fact be given a run like a play. I quite concurred, but the editor, Algernon Locker, was not impressed by the proposal. Lucas was soon promoted to write short leaders on light topics, and then to produce the Saturday *Literary Gossip* column.   In this job, after some years, I succeeded him, and I mention it because I want to tell him something which apparently he does not know.   While I was "Gossiping," Lucas acted sometimes as reader to a certain publisher, and in this connection he confesses to one of his worst blunders in this branch of his career.   "Having, in 1910, an early copy of Stephen Leacock's *Literary Lapses* in the first Canadian edition, I wrote an enthusiastic article on it, but neglected to mention it to my employer.   John Lane, having read the article, at once secured the English rights, and the author has remained with the Lane firm ever since." It happened that I, too, had written enthusiastically of Leacock's book, and in the very column I had taken over from Lucas.   John Lane read my paragraphs and wrote to me; then he cabled to Stephen Leacock, with the result that he secured a most valuable connection.   I had ploughed for him with Lucas's heifer.   The *Globe* enabled my old friend to open his first banking account, and it is he who now recalls that I was the first person for whom he drew a cheque.   It was indeed the first in his virgin cheque-book and was for a million pounds.   He correctly adds that I did not present it but had it framed.   What he does not relate is that a few weeks later, when we were walking on a dark evening up Highgate Hill, I noticed the branch bank where his account lay was lit up, and remarked: 'What is your bank doing at this time?'   He looked and growled sadly: 'I expect they're trying to find my balance.'"

In this letter I am afraid there is as much of what I remember as of what Lucas remembers, but that is as much his fault as mine.   And many unused notes of both confront me still.

[*September* 24, 1932.]

WHAT IS GREAT POETRY?*

I AM too wary to ask What is Poetry? or What is a Poet? for I should then involve myself in unfruitful discussion. If you were to stop a stranger in the street (with the right sort of smile) and ask him, What is Poetry? he would probably answer, "The Opposite of Prose," and leave you standing. His definition would amount to precisely nothing. Poetry is not the opposite to Prose, it is a thing so entirely itself as to have no opposite. In any case, its opposite is not prose, any more than the opposite of a rose is a rose-bush. Even the great dictionaries define poetry in like manner, that is to say in terms of form, not of spirit—metrical language, patterned arrangement of words, and what not. They tell us little to the purpose. When the man-in-the-street sees a composition printed in short lines and divided into sections, called verses, he recognises it as "poetry," and there is no need to quarrel with his useful but inexact phrase. The New English Dictionary acknowledges, in fact, that poetry in its simplest and lowest form is just versification or verse. How good or bad the verses are does not here matter. Some bad poetry is bad enough to be pathetically good, and at least one anthology of this sort has been compiled in recent years for our entertainment. Andrew Lang, who was equally a humorist and a critic, said that the very best-worst lines he had received for private criticism were these—they were the last in a ballad about a lady of colour who was concluding her first and not too happy visit to England:—

> And now the time has come to leave her,
> Far from where her swarthy kindred roam,
> In the Scarlet Fever, Scarlet Fever,
> Scarlet Fever Convalescent Home.

* Being incomplete notes for an address to "John o' London's" Literary Circle, London Centre.

It is not my intention to trace the upward trend of poetry from this level.

Nevertheless, the simpler (really the more difficult) question cannot be evaded. How did poetry originate? I got my first answer to this question when, as a schoolboy in York, I listened to that unrivalled University Extension lecturer, Professor R. G. Moulton, in a hall within the beautiful grounds of St. Mary's Abbey. Shortly, he said, poetry sprang from the war dance. Thus do the graces of life spring from its brutalities. But the theory seems sound. The war dance begat strange war cries just as colleges still evolve their college cries. The war cry naturally became as rhythmical as the dance and—Poetry was born.

Obviously, I cannot even begin to trace the development of Poetry from the primitive war cry to Milton's *Lycidas*; I am not competent to do what, in fact, has never been done. But I will draw your attention to two very old elements which account in part for that development and which still persist among the graces of poetry, even the highest. The first is that familiar device, Alliteration, which, as you know, is the use of the same consonant or vowel sound at the beginning of two or more words which are in juxtaposition. An extreme, and not inspired, example of Alliteration is that old "Reciter" piece beginning:—

> An Austrian army awfully arrayed
> Boldly by battering besieged Belgrade,
> Cossack commanders cannonading come,
> Dealing destruction's devastating doom . . .

and so it goes on through the letters of the alphabet. It is a mere literary curiosity, but it illustrates the meaning and working of Alliteration. A far higher example is Coleridge's verse in *The Ancient Mariner*:—

> The fair breeze blew, the white foam flew,
> The furrow followed free;
> We were the first that ever burst
> Into that silent sea.

But alliteration is more subtle and effective when it is not confined to the beginnings of words but is allowed to permeate a line less conspicuously. A good example is Tennyson's:—

> The moan of doves in immemorial elms,
> And murmur of innumerable bees.

Alliteration has been well described as the jingle which tends to impose itself on language, whether verse or prose, as in "spick and span," "weal and woe," and so on. Its highest uses have been discovered by the greater poets.

The second primitive element in poetry to which I have referred is called by the rather formidable Greek name, Onomatopœia, though another name for it is Echoism. The simple meaning is that sound is made to imitate sense. Thus *flop*, *crash* and *bang* are onomatopœic words and in a higher way *thunder*, *ripple* and *whisper*. Tennyson's line about the bees that I have just quoted is both alliterative and onomatopœic and the two devices usually if not always strengthen each other. Some of the Latin poets were masters of onomatopœia, though they did not use alliteration—Virgil in particular. He has a hexameter line which wonderfully imitates the sound of the hoofs of a cavalry regiment approaching a camp on a hard road; another which reproduces in its sound the stunning of an ox by a butcher—and so forth, though he can use onomatopœia to describe not a material sight or sound, but even a mood—as of rapture or despair—the highest use to which onomatopœia is put in great poetry. It is perhaps never so effective as when it is too subtle to be recognised. To give an example on the spur of the moment—Milton has this in his *Il Penseroso*:—

> Oft on a plat of rising ground,
> I hear the far off curfew sound,
> Over some wide water'd shore,
> Swinging slow with sullen roar.

The last two lines are most delicately onomatopœic. What a sense of still distance in "wide water'd shore"! and if you doubt the propriety of describing the sound of a distant bell as a *sullen roar* I am afraid I must suggest that you can never have listened in the same circumstances. Milton's phrase is very truth.

It may be said that all this is concerned with the body rather than with the soul of poetry. But body and soul are as much united in a work of art as in the man who produced it, and you cannot understand one without the other; therefore, even in these almost random jottings I wish to include both. When, however, I come to the soul of poetry and to ask, "In what does *great* poetry consist?" I despair of giving a direct answer. I doubt whether one can be given. Where to begin? We cannot afford time to compare bad poetry with good. Let us try to compare good poetry with better, and better with best. To do it at all, one must select three passages of poetry which are written in like vein and, as far as possible, on the same theme; it will be well, also, if these passages are familiar so that there is no newness to distract or delay judgment. Well, then, take three stanzas from the poem which, of all others in our literature, has satisfied the average man and woman. I refer to Gray's *Elegy* and to these stanzas:—

> The boast of heraldry, the pomp of power,
> And all that beauty, all that wealth e'er gave,
> Awaits alike th' inevitable hour:—
> The paths of glory lead but to the grave.

Nor you, ye proud, impute to these the fault
If memory o'er their tombs no trophies raise,
Where through the long-drawn aisle and fretted vault
The pealing anthem swells the note of praise.

Can storied urn, or animated bust,
Back to its mansion call the fleeting breath?
Can honour's voice provoke the silent dust,
Or flattery soothe the dull cold ear of death?

Noble poetry, you say. I agree. But we are just now
concerned with the comparative heights to which poets
rise, and I am going to suggest that a hundred years before
Gray had written these lines another poet, also not of the
highest rank, had written lines under a like inspiration
which are on a higher plane of poetic art. I refer to
James Shirley and his beautiful poem *Death the Leveller*,
These are the first and last of its three stanzas:—

> The glories of our blood and state
>   Are shadows, not substantial things;
> There is no armour against fate ;
>   Death lays his icy hand on kings.
>   Sceptre and Crown
>   Must tumble down,
> And in the dust be equal made
> With the poor crookèd scythe and spade.
>
> The garlands wither on your brow,
>   Then boast no more your mighty deeds,
> Upon Death's purple altar now,
>   See where the victor-victim bleeds!
>   Your heads must come
>   To the cold tomb,
> Only the actions of the just
> Smell sweet and blossom in the dust.

Is there not here a larger note, a more majestical sweep, a
deeper cadence? I submit that there is, but I do not
ask you to agree. Thirdly, I transcribe the last sad speech
of Prospero from *The Tempest*:—

And like the baseless fabric of this vision,
The cloud-capped towers, the gorgeous palaces,
The solemn temples, the great globe itself,
Yea, all which it inherit, shall dissolve
And like an unsubstantial pageant faded
Leave not a wrack behind.   We are such stuff
As dreams are made on, and our little life
Is rounded with a sleep.

Gray writes a noble and studied epitaph on the humble
and lowly of heart, Shirley warns the mighty in their seats,
but Shakespeare's lines are a requiem on Man himself and
on all the cities of the earth and the glory of them.   Each
of the three, but Shakespeare most, convinces me that a
great line of poetry is the greatest of human achievements.

[*October* 8, 1932.]

MUSIC AND MUSIC

FOR me Music is the greatest mystery under the sun.
It may have been so to Handel, Wagner, and to the
man who played on the triangle last night—I don't know.
I can understand as well as most, perhaps, the way of an
eagle in the air, the way of a ship on the sea, and even the
way of a man with a maid, but this is saying little, because
the wisest of men confessed that these things were too
wonderful for him.   What I do not understand at all is the
way of a boy with a tin whistle, or, for that matter, without
one.   Like Charles Lamb, "I have no ear."   But like him
I can add: "To say that this heart never melted at the
concord of sweet sounds, would be a foul self-libel. . . .   I
even think that *sentimentally* I am disposed to harmony.
But *organically* I am incapable of a tune.   I have been
practising *God Save the King* all my life; whistling and hum-

ming of it over to myself in solitary corners; and am not
yet arrived, they tell me, within many quavers of it.   Yet
hath the loyalty of Elia never been impeached." · Nor hath
mine.   But it took me many years to recognise the National
Anthem aurally; I had to rely on the removal of hats.
Even now, it is the only musical composition that I know
without the words.   Orchestrate *Auld Lang Syne* with
"variations" and I should not be wise to it, although
I have "sung" its *words* (heaven forgive me!) these fifty
years.   This is not the whole tragedy.   For Elia, with a
prescience of my state, goes on: "I am not without suspicion,
that I have an undeveloped faculty of music within me.
For thrumming, in my wild way, on my friend A.'s piano,
the other morning, while he was engaged in an adjoining
parlour—on his return he was pleased to say, *he thought
it could not be the maid!*"   What A. probably meant (he
would have meant it in my case) was, that he could have
sworn it was the cat.   But Elia leaps to a nobler conclusion:

> A grace, snatched from a superior refinement, soon
> convinced him that some being—technically perhaps
> deficient, but higher informed from a principle common
> to all the fine arts—had swayed the keys to a mood
> which *Jenny*, with all her (less cultivated) enthusiasm,
> could never have elicited from them.

"Swayed the keys!"—O the Mozart in me!   Have I not in
railway carriages and on lonely roads lifted up my voice
in thunder and sighing and Orphean flutings and golden
swells and bagpipe wails, imagining myself

> Bowzybeus, who could sweetly sing
> Or with the rosin'd bow torment the string!

How does Sir Landon Ronald, how does Mr. Jack Hylton,
know what they may have lost in my impromptu *motifs*
and vocal amoks?   They do not know—nor I.

Musicians have cornered music.   They think it is all an

affair of notes, tootlings, major thirds, arias, Brahms (what
are brahms?), crotchets, debussies, counterpoints, batons,
Albert Hall psychology, and an absent master's voice.
Actually the Greek word from which we take our own
was applied to all the arts of the Nine Muses, including
history, astronomy, mathematics and, if you please, poetry.
Not all "music" is instrumental or even in the concert-
hall sense vocal; it is perhaps never nobler than when it
is merely verbal. And the strange thing—I, at least,
cannot understand it—is that musicians are not often poets
and poets not often musicians. As often as not the two
musics are unrelated. Or are they? Mr. Laurence
Binyon, who is retiring from the British Museum after
forty years' service to take up the Professorship of Poetry
at Harvard University, knows a great deal about the one
music and next to nothing about the other. I read, in the
Morning Post: "He is one of those curious instances of a
man more than ordinarily sensitive, as a poet, to the music
of words, who is at the same time utterly indifferent to
music itself. This was the case with Tennyson, Browning,
and Swinburne." Although the writer describes this
instance of limitation as "curious," he promptly gives
three similar instances showing that it is not so curious
after all. And what does he really mean by "music itself"?
Confusion arises from our use of the same word for two
experiences which we commonly regard as quite separate.
Perhaps they are really separate, though it is difficult to
think so, and still more difficult to think of them as one.
"Utterly indifferent to music itself," Mr. Binyon could
yet write these exquisitely cadenced lines in his after-War
poem, *For the Fallen*:—

> They shall grow not old, as we that are left grow old:
> Age shall not weary them, nor the years condemn.
> At the going down of the sun and in the morning
> We will remember them.

They mingle not with their laughing comrades again;
They sit no more at familiar tables at home;
They have no lot in our labour of the daytime;
They sleep beyond England's foam.

But where our desires are and our hopes profound,
Felt as a well-spring that is hidden from sight,
To the innermost heart of their own land they are known
As the stars are known to the Night.

I will swear there is here more "music itself" (rightly
voiced) than in most of the stuff with which the B.B.C.
torments the ether. Tell me, sons and daughters of
Apollo, how it is that a poet to whom good music makes
"no appeal whatever" can be thus musical, and how I,
in like case, can yield to the spell?

Lest you try to put me off with some subtlety about
songs sung and songs unsung, and argue, perhaps, that
the unsung song is only half a song, I remind you that there
is a music of prose as well as of poetry, and then it may be
my turn to be over-subtle. How is it that Charles Lamb,
who did not know one musical note from another, could
write the last paragraph of his essay, *Amicus Redivivus*,
in which he describes his rescue of his learned and simple-
minded friend, George Dyer, from the New River, outside
Colebrooke Cottage at Islington. He represents that he
had snatched G. D. from the next world, and had even
disappointed it by so few seconds that:—

A pulse assuredly was felt along the line of the Elysian
shades, when the near arrival of G. D. was announced
by no equivocal indications. From their seats of
Asphodel arose the gentler and the graver ghosts—
poet or historian of Grecian or of Roman lore—to
crown with unfading chaplets the half-finished love-
labours of their unwearied scholiast. Him Markland
expected—him Tyrwhitt hoped to encounter—him the
sweet lyrist of Peter House, whom he had barely seen

upon earth, with newest airs prepared to greet; and, patron of the gentle Christ's boy—who should have been his patron for life—the mild Askew, with longing aspirations, leaned foremost from his venerable Æsculapian chair, to welcome into that happy company the matured virtues of the man, whose tender scions in the boy he himself upon earth had so prophetically fed and watered. There, I submit, you have a music of prose beautifully attuned and sustained by a man who had not "ear" enough to catch the notes of *God Save the King*. If "music itself" is mysterious, the mystery must be shared. The only great English poet I can think of who was definitely a musician is Milton, and I have always thought that he must have written the slow, swelling, soul-laden opening (call it overture) of *Paradise Lost* after trying it, somehow, on his organ. But could Handel have carried it further?

[*March* 25, 1933.]

T. P.*

MY old friend and employer, "the one and only T. P.," as Lord Curzon of Kedleston called him, had a trick of opening any personal sketch he was writing with the words: "The first time I ever saw——." It was a good gambit because it aroused curiosity and satisfied it almost in the same instant. Yet I think I can beat it here, for with hardly a stretch of truth I can say that I saw T. P. for the first time twice. And if I do not now see my old master in yet a new light it is because Mr. Hamilton Fyfe's memories and impressions of Thomas Power O'Connor agree so closely with my own. What is much

* *T. P. O'Connor*, by Hamilton Fyfe (Allen & Unwin, 16*s*.).

more important is that Mr. Fyfe has written his biography
in exactly the tone and spirit which T. P. himself, I am
convinced, would have desired. It is informal, frank,
inter-human.

The first time I ever saw T. P. was at a super-heated
Irish Home Rule demonstration in Newcastle Town Hall.
He sat on the platform, I in the far-back gallery. He had
come from London, the House of Commons, the centre of
things; I, from putting up the shutters of a tea-dealer's
shop. I was there more for fun than anything else; for in
those mid-years of the 'eighties a Home Rule meeting was
likely to provide red-hot eloquence and even Donnybrook
Fair entertainment. The only other celebrity on the platform I can recall was the hunch-backed Mr. Biggar, who
had often talked the House of Commons blind (he once
spoke for four hours) as the original Obstructionist, who
had turned the Prince of Wales (King Edward VII) out
of the Peers' Gallery by "spying strangers," and who now
sat next to T. P. like a self-communing toad. He was
the perfect foil of his neighbour, the *beau sabreur* of politics,
on whose raven hair and vivid presence my gaze was
mostly fixed. After hearing T. P.'s speech, resonant as a
trumpet, how could I know, how dream, that one day I
should work familiarly with him in London?

I did not see him again for about eighteen years. Then,
one day, on my coming in from lunch to the *Academy*
office in Chancery Lane, my chief (Lewis Hind) said:
"T. P. O'Connor wants to see you." I went, in a daze, to
the office of *M.A.P.*, where the godlike orator of the Town
Hall platform, now an editor and journalist of almost
world-wide fame, pointed to a chair and said in his soft
Irish tones: "Mr. ——, I have heard of you." Thus
began a ten years' connection, and thus *T.P.'s Weekly* came
into being. There is a first floor bow window in Northumberland Avenue, opposite the Grand Hotel, at which I

was soon talking shop with T. P. in the new paper's office. I had much to learn of his aims and ideas, but he summed these up to my satisfaction, and not a little to my terror, when in one of these early talks he said in the smooth Athlone brogue that never left him, "Mr. ———, I see no reason in the wur-r-r-ld why *every line* in this paper should not thra-arb with human int'rist." There he spoke from his heart; human interest was his spiritual food. He was even haunted by the misgiving that journalism was not his true line, because it was concerned so greatly with events in which, he once declared, he was far less interested than most people. "The matters that really interest me in life are not passing events but abiding passions and problems." And Mr. Fyfe's comment is just right:—

That this was a sound reading of his own mind is proved by incidents of which many examples could be given. Here is one. Going to a political meeting, he read *Beauchamp's Career* in the train and was so absorbed in the story, the first of Meredith's he had tried, that he "forgot all about the small and apparently trivial things on which I was to speak." He envied Meredith's reputation. They became friends. When a body of authors visited the novelist on some anniversary occasion, he made T. P. sit next to him and they had, after the ceremony, good talk. T. P. was in accord with Meredith's appeal to him to "believe in a hearty God—one to love more than to fear"; in agreement too, with his assurance on this occasion that "only by conquering the fear of death can you possess your life."

Meredith's achievement seemed to T. P. wholly enviable, his own he belittled. "What I should like to have done with my life I have never done."

The main reason for T. P.'s failure, against his own ambition, to express himself and to explore "human interest" in the broader medium of books, instead of in newspaper columns, is given by Mr. Fyfe in a sentence: "He lived in perpetual need of money."

Money passed through T. P.'s hands like water. He was lavishly generous to others, but himself seemed to be always or, at any rate, at inevitably recurring periods, oppressed by "that eternal want of pence which vexes public men." This was the goad that drove him, and kept him, on the road of journalism. There he could be sure of making money. Apart from the high value of his journalistic work and his capacity for turning it out in volume, T. P. was a past-master in getting high payment and making good bargains. His Parliamentary fame, his knowledge of the world and its personalities, his abounding geniality and wealth of experience made him *persona grata* everywhere. His persuasiveness, though never overdone, was hypnotic, and capitalists and directors fell to it easily, though not permanently. Truth to tell, he milked his financial kine too hard. He was a great creative journalist, but never a sound commercial one, and paper after paper slowly wilted in his hands. His need of money pushed him ever forward, but always from one enterprise to another. Mr. Fyfe says: "Always writing under the pressure of this need, he was unable to do work of lasting value; the other kind could be produced so much more quickly and could be sold at a higher price. Yet, although as a writer of books he made no reputation, as editor he left his mark upon the history of the newspaper. He was a pioneer of the new journalism, not on the commercial, but on the editorial side." But, through it all, T. P. was faithful—he could not be otherwise—to his basic belief in "human interest."

Describing his plans for his first great achievement, the *Star*, Mr. Fyfe writes of its arrival:—

Then came the earliest stone flung at the Old Journalism, almost purely political in character: "We believe that the reader of the daily journal longs for other

M

reading than mere politics." He longed also for less
inflated, less conventional phrasing. In reporting news
the *Star* would "do away with the hackneyed style of
obsolete journalism," there would be "no place in it
for the verbose and prolix articles to which most of our
contemporaries still adhere." These promises were kept.
T. P. was the first editor in British journalism to impress
upon his staff the value of "the human side" and the
personal note. After him the insistence upon this may
have grown mechanical and stupid or recklessly sensational. But in his hands these elements added to the
newspaper a new and to most people a welcome feature.
He sensed the existence of a new public. While North-
cliffe was still at school, T. P. was planning a journal
that should shine and give out warmth, should both
sparkle and enlighten. He was a rebel against the
chilly dullness of the Press at that time. In a *New
Review* article he declared his belief that "the public
suffered more from the cowardice than from the audacity
of journalism, from the suppression rather than the
publication of awkward facts." He maintained that
"everything which can be talked about can be written
about."

That last remark must not be misunderstood: T. P.'s
boldness was never indiscreet or his realism offensive.

I do not think that T. P. missed his true sphere as a writer.
He was not a literary artist, nor more than an *ad hoc* philosopher. It was said by a great critic of Byron that when
he reflected he was lost. T. P. was always too near to
fact and personality to develop wide views; his was not a
really reflective mind. But his genius for presenting
character with a *punch* was unique. When, in 1898, he
brought out *M.A.P.* under the firm of Arthur Pearson,
he wrote:—

This journal will be purely personal. I shall write,

not about politics, but about politicians; not about
books, but about their authors; not about finance, but
about financiers; not of plays, but of playwrights; not
of acting, but of actors.

If this was not the highest form of journalism it stood, he
maintained, in no need of apology.   In any case he practised
it better than anyone else.   For the kind of writing which
finds its natural expression in the essay he had little taste.
For fanciful, discursive matter he had his own amusing
word of disparagement; he called it "filigree."   His almost
physical grasp of personality and personal drama could
not be imitated.   Not, certainly, by me.   At the close of
the Boer War he asked me for some quite unusual reason
to write a page in *T.P.'s Weekly* on the tragedy of Kruger.
It was not my subject, but I did my best, and thought it
well to submit the result to his approval.   He gently
shook his head and, for reply, took away my article,
re-wrote it, and handed me his own version.   It was T. P.
at his best, and beyond my envy.

[*February* 3, 1934.]

HOW MAD WAS HE?*

A BOOK could be written to prove that the world
owes more to its reputed madmen than to its reputed
wise men.   The Athenians thought Socrates was mad.
The Jews thought that Jesus of Nazareth was mad.   In
mediæval Italy they called Galileo mad.   Cervantes made
Don Quixote's madness a vehicle of wisdom.   Cowper's
madness never got into his poetry; William Blake's got

* *The Eccentric Life of Alexander Cruden*, by Edith Olivier (Faber & Faber
12s. 6d.).

into his poetry and made it great.   Among the innumerable minor madmen to whom the world is indebted Alexander Cruden has his place.   Just how mad he was is not easy to say, though it was his lot to be confined in three private lunatic asylums.   Miss Olivier's title page is in some degree a contradiction in terms, for it asserts only Cruden's eccentricity, while above it appears a reproduction of Cibber's sculpture of two madmen which adorned (or disfigured) the entrance to the original Bedlam, an institution which never knew Cruden and would probably not have accepted him as a patient.   Yet Cruden could not possibly be described as "normal."   He may more safely be described as one of God's fools.

To the world he is known, not by his eccentricities but by his *Complete Concordance of the Old and New Testaments*. Few more prodigious works have been carried out by one man.   Yet it is said (I, for one, cannot believe it) that he produced his colossal multiple index of the Bible in little more than a year.   In his preface he explained that:—

A Concordance is a Dictionary, or an Index, to the Bible, wherein all the words used through the inspired writings are arranged alphabetically, and the various places where they occur are referred to, to assist us in finding our passages, and comparing the several significations of the same word.

Cruden's *Concordance* was not the first of its kind—more than twenty such already existed—but by its fulness and science it superseded all these and has never itself been superseded.   It is so complete that, as the author of this biography says, only one or two omissions have been detected.   "Even Cruden's fine mesh was evaded by *Huz*, the brother of Buz; while it may have been an instinctive reaction from the implied effeminacy which made him omit the '*powders* of the merchants' with which the bridegroom perfumed himself in the Song of Solomon."   The will to keep his nose on the grindstone was one of Cruden's strong points, and largely accounts for his single-handed achievement. But this was not all. In his Aberdeen home, where godliness and Calvinism reigned, he had in childhood become a keen reader of the Bible, if only in a way suited to his years. A kind of Bible-reading game was then popular in such homes. It consisted in selecting a particular word, and then looking for it in chapter after chapter and Book after Book, noting its occurrences and finally counting them up. This Bible word game was played either alone or in competition; it may be that it or similar ones are played still. (As a schoolboy I invented one for myself. It was collecting *ites*. There are no end of them in the Pentateuch, and on Sunday afternoons, when we read our Bibles under compulsion, I revelled among the Amalekites, the Hivites, the Jebusites and all the rest.) Alexander was the first Cruden to become famous, and the last. It was in the winter of 1736 that the little London City bookseller (such he had become) sat down to his huge undertaking, which for him "was no drudgery, but a sustained passion of delight."

In his Royal Exchange bookshop, toiling all day between the calls of customers, Cruden became lost in his task. He finished the *Concordance* in the winter of 1737 and dedicated it to George II's Queen (Caroline of Anspach), a woman of high culture to whom he was already "Queen's Book-seller" by royal warrant. She allowed Cruden personally to present her with a copy of the work at St. James's Palace. There she talked to him pleasantly, said she was "mightily obliged" and promised to reward him with a grant of £100 from her privy purse. But a few weeks later came the Queen's sudden death, and Cruden did not receive his money, which, at that time, he sorely needed. He felt, however, that he had produced a work that would "bless the world," boasted himself "Apothecary to the

Parsons," and was never tired of repeating the praise of ministers, one of whom told him that "the Bible and this *Concordance* taught him to preach." The usefulness of the work is, indeed, beyond praise; with its aid any imperfectly remembered Bible phrase or passage can be found. As Miss Olivier says, if you want to look up a reference in the Bible, you must have Cruden's *Concordance* at your elbow. This is the sole purpose of the work, "wherein (he said) a required text may be found by looking out any material word, whether it be substantive, adjective, verb, etc." In using it, much time can be saved by selecting as the clue a word which is not likely to be frequent in the Bible. For example, one may wish to recall that fine passage: "He hath showed thee, O man, what is good; and what doth the Lord require of thee, but to do justly, and to love mercy, and to walk humbly with thy God?" It is obvious that words like "man," "good," "mercy," "walk," and "God" must occur hundreds of times in the Bible. Select, therefore, a word less likely to be recurrent; in this instance "require" would, if remembered, give the passage (Micah vi, 8) more quickly than any other, though "humbly" and "justly," being adverbs, much less frequent then "humble" and "just," would serve well. Miss Olivier says: "Cruden's *Concordance* is not amusing reading; it contains too little Cruden." That little is to be found chiefly in the "Significations," as he calls them, which he attaches to certain words, usually names of natural objects. His notes on Bible birds, beasts, and fishes leave one gasping. He believes that *Swallows* in winter live under water "wherein sometimes great lumps of swallows have been fished up, fixed to one another by the claws and beak." *Hornets* he describes as:—

A sort of strong flies which the Lord used as instruments to plague the enemies of his people. They are of themselves very troublesome and mischievous, but those the Lord made use of were, it is thought, like the flies wherewith he plagued Egypt, of an extraordinary bigness and perniciousness. It is said they live as the wasps, that they have a king or captain, and pestilent stings as bees, and that if twenty-seven of them sting man or beast, it is certain death to either.

Considering its great success, and that three editions appeared in his lifetime, the *Concordance* brought its author only moderate reward. In twenty-three years it yielded him little more than £40 a year.

Cruden's most permanent occupation was that of the corrector of the press; he was probably the best proof-reader of his time. But about the year 1753 he began to style himself "Corrector" in another sense. He conceived that from correcting proofs he was called to assume the mission and title of Corrector of the Morals of the Nation. In London he saw everywhere "polluting Playhouses, monstrous Masquerades and pernicious Cardplaying." He saw great folks travelling on the Sabbath, and thousands going for walks. With his own eyes he had seen a clergy-man of the Church of England profane the Lord's Day by taking the air on the terrace at Windsor. Such were the evils, says his present biographer, which made Cruden resolve that Alexander the Proof-Corrector must become Alexander the Corrector of Morals. Here we approach Alexander the Mad, though in truth he was never more than amiably and benevolently mad. Miss Olivier tells the story with wit and sympathy, and with such art that I do not hesitate to compare her description of Cruden's escape from Mr. Wright's Madhouse in Bethnal Green with the best passages of Defoe. Thrice he suffered all that the ignorant and infamous madhouse system of the period could inflict on men and women who had the courage to be unusual and the misfortune to be in the way.

Each of Cruden's confinements in an asylum coincided

with a love affair, and Miss Olivier is probably right when she suggests that he was never so mad as in the last of these episodes. The lady's name was Elizabeth Abney; she was the daughter of Sir Thomas Abney, who had been Lord Mayor of London in the reigns of William III and Queen Anne. When he conceived his passion for Miss Abney the Corrector had not so much as seen her. While it continued he never saw her—nor afterwards. He loved, so to speak, *in vacuo*, yet expected the lady's hand as "a gift from Heaven." Nor did he neglect romantic conventions. Even as Spenser had hailed his Queen, not by her own name, but as Gloriana Belphœbe; even as the Knight of the rueful countenance had beatified his wench as the Donna Maria Dulcinea del Toboso: so did the Corrector, scorning Abney, bestow on his Lady the lustrous name— WHITAKER. And when after a year of fruitless letter-writing and door-knocking he resigned hope, his letter of farewell bore that celestial cognomen.

On November 1st, 1770, the Corrector, Concordance-maker, Bookseller, Lover, and Lunatic failed to appear at breakfast in Camden Street, Islington. He was found in the powdering closet, his hands clasped, his head upon an open Bible, dead.

[*May* 26, 1934.]

ON GOING BACK

TO revisit one's birthplace is, for man or woman, an adventure. But if that place, besides being the accidental site of our entry, became the background of our growth and of our initiation into the wide world—above all, if it was the scene of our first, last, indescribable encounter with all Being (though the blinding vision may have come at some petty street corner) then our return to the old town, the old village, may well be called an adventure of the soul. If it does not prove so, if disillusion comes, it is because we forget that the soul, pregnant with celestial fire, is equally itself in every time and every place. The soul does not go visiting. Has the butterfly any wish to re-enter its chrysalis shell? Yet in men and women the "return of the native" instinct is strong, often compelling. Whether it become a vivid spiritual experience is for the individual to know—and to recount if he pleases.

Dr. Johnson's penitential return to Lichfield, where he stood silent and bare-headed in the market-place to purge an early grieving of his father, has to do with his character, not with my present theme. More to the point is his playfully caustic essay on the return of Serotinus to his native town. You will find it in his *Rambler*, No. 165, written in October, 1751. Serotinus himself describes his adventurous, but not soulful, pilgrimage after spending all his working years in getting reputation and getting money. He relies on his success for a great reception. To dazzle his old townsmen and neighbours he puts his servants into new livery and orders a new chariot. While these are making ready he ponders what his tone and behaviour shall be, and is quick to see that he must vary them according as he is greeted with reverence or with awkward respect,

or with envy or flippancy, or mendicant fawning. Whenever he is congratulated on his career in London he must
remember to hint that his success was only what he
expected—and deserved. Having sent casual word of his
coming, he at last enters the town in state. The roll of
his carriage, and his horses' hoofs on the cobbles, bring
many people to their doors and windows, but only to stare.
Then an old acquaintance—the barber—rushes to his side
and greets him as in the old days. Serotinus, not quite
sure of his code, is haughtily polite, whereupon the barber
damns him and retreats to his shop. Within an hour
Serotinus sees things as they are: "no smoke of bonfires, no
harmony of bells, no shout of crowds, nor riot of joy."
After ordering a splendid dinner at his inn for old friends,
he sits down to it alone and leaves it untasted in his chagrin.
But his disappointment brings wisdom, and his final
reflection has an appositeness to all "homing" absentees:—

> Of the friends whose compliments I expected, some
> had long ago moved to distant provinces, some had lost
> in the maladies of age all sense of another's prosperity,
> and some had forgotten our former intimacy amidst
> care and distresses. . . . All those whom I loved, feared,
> or hated, all whose envy or whose kindness I had hopes
> of contemplating with pleasure, were swept away, and
> their place was filled by a new generation with other
> views and other competitions.

The truth is that *going back* is a queer, salutary, humbling
experience, productive of sardonic humour and a sadness
(without depression) all its own.

Between the old native returned, and the young one
on the spot, there can be few exchanges. Except as a map,
as a topographical pattern, they see the town with different
eyes and very different reactions. A's is not B's town any
more than 1935 is 1875. In Rye Hill I looked up at a top-
storey window. Through that window, from my small

bed, I used to see a red glow from the foundries where cannon were made. Its pulsations on the night sky would keep me awake and fearful. For they gave the impression of *approaching* Fire; and in a childish unreasoned way I connected those Elswick flames with the eternal ones of a larger establishment. It seems unlikely, indeed not credible, that a Tyneside child of to-day would see that nightly illumination in that way, or that even its parents carry about such a memory. Passing Elswick East Terrace I looked down it wondering whether I should see a strange brown shape, in a lurking attitude, which once held me ready to flee. I had for the first time seen a dancing bear in some street and it was in my head that the monster, no longer held by chain and cudgel, was now a potential devourer of well-fed children. Do bears dance on Tyneside to-day? In Bentinck Road, who but I had a thought for the holly tree up which I was lifted in grandmotherly arms to look into my first bird's-nest? Twenty-five years ago it was there—now only its place is there. But it lives in the soil of memory.

To ramble a town with both the knowledge of a native and the detachment of a stranger is a curious experience. I could fancy myself invisible in these new crowds; there was no barber to shatter the illusion. Almost I resented their presence in the precincts of my early self-consciousness —I had almost written self-importance. Against that old background even motor-cars seemed like new inventions to one who remembered Dalmatian hounds running behind family carriages in these very streets when they were Victorian. Velocipedes, too, the height of a man. Soldiers in shakos. Now and then a mad bull. Boys and girls running barefoot in mud or frost—their rags accepted as in the order of things and as a sufficient reason for "Ragged Schools." I could spare some of these things, others were sheer loss. What the devil does this upstart generation

mean by clearing away my jolly old cattle market with its
hundreds of wooden pens? Where now are the big men
in big hats, with cunning sticks, who seemed to talk inter-
minably about nothing until an arm was raised heavenward
as in ritual, and then one straightened palm descending,
met another—*smack!*—the bargain was sealed and a score
of washed pigs no wiser. All that acreage of bleat and
bristle gone—to be a place of irrelevant garages. From
this pillage of my young heart I turned to look for the
studio to which we were brought to stand white-socked and
super-brushed in front of a man with a shawl over his head
after he had fixed our own heads in machines that did not
show in the family album. Gone!—a meaningless travel
bureau had replaced that Temple of the *Carte-de-visite*. I
was somewhat restored by seeing the old letters, F. P.,
on a near house. Not your meagre London H, as who
should say Hydrant when FIRE PLUG offered.

After a generation or more one cannot go back to what
we quitted: it is not there. Hence such returns are more
interesting than emotional. The hearth remains, the fire is
out. My old Newcastle was rough and racy, dirty and
drunken, happy in itself, and in its own humour and songs,
and convinced that "There's nee place like Wa-a-ker."
But as I saw the Town become a City I have now seen the
City become a metropolis. Even the local accent is diluted
nearly to normal; even the old Tyneside words—even
"canny"—eluded me in the "canny toon," until in an
evening paper I read that a street bookmaker, on being
arrested by the police, had remarked blithely: "Well, it's
gone a canny time." Yet there is not a little left of modern
antiquity—the antiquity of one's own period. I found it
in the humpy granite setts and garden railings of Summerhill
Grove; in Eldon Place, where lived George and Robert
Stephenson; and in Ashfield Terrace West, where my last
school dame awarded me a copy of *Paul and Virginia* and

rashly inscribed it "for proficiency in all his studies"; I keep it still—to save the mark.

It was at lonely little Wetheral, over the Cumberland border, that I looked up at eight or nine firs and cypresses that I had helped my father to plant when they were ten to fifteen feet high. Some were now little short of forty feet; one, I think, is nearly fifty feet up. A tall, grizzled man came into the hotel bar parlour where I was sitting alone—looked at me rather intently—and said: "I think you are a ——," giving my surname. In amazement I asked how he guessed it. "Resemblance," he said briefly. He was not sure that he had ever seen me, but he had known my family and even named a younger brother. It was something, after fifty years, and by the accident of an accident, to be recognised even as a species. But thus we must melt away. I had just found after long search in the churchyard, where the noonday stillness was broken only by the murmur of the Eden over its rocks, the small gravestone on which I had, as a hobble-de-hoy, read:—

> In this vain world short was my stay,
>   And empty was my laughter,
> I go before to lead the way
>   And thou comes jogging after.

How easy it is for the dead to poke fun at the living!

"Aye farewell, and then for ever . . ." is, I guess, a good rule. I think I have said it, and for ever. Beautiful City, "Pride of the North"—long and loftily may your great Church, your black Keep, and your classic Moot Hall look steeply on the river that brings romance down from the Border to the sea. Farewell to all that.

[*October* 19, 1935.]

THE SIDESEA EQUATION

A FEW evenings ago, in a tea-shop at Sidesea (technic-
ally it was not a tea-shop), I observed a lady of the
people busy at a table. She was using a fountain-pen with
an urgency which somehow, in the surroundings, suggested
postcards. And postcards they were, for their three-
colour gaiety reached me at ten yards' distance. Her
husband seemed to be looking on in placid approval.

The situation was of course familiar, but for some reason,
or for no reason, I began to ponder the matter. The
"beached margent" of the sea is to-day a gallery of picture-
postcards. They flash upon that outer eye which is *not* the
bliss of solitude. Always they are different and always
they are the same. Ninety-five per cent are unsurpassably
vulgar; the remaining five per cent are apt to vex the clergy.
I am not going to moralise about either class, but only, if
I can, to account for their inescapable actuality. What
struck me most was the sender's enthusiasm and then,
through her, the magnitude of this vogue. If it be thought
that the subject is unworthy of attention, I can but plead in
those famous words which brought down the house in
a Roman theatre, *Homo sum; humani nihil a me alienum puto*:
"I am a man and nothing that concerns mankind is indifferent to me." It is not the impulse but the medium that
invites a little inquiry. After all, these *fortissimo* messages
carry kindness and high spirits back to town as surely as
"There's rosemary, that's for remembrance . . . and there
is pansies, that's for thoughts." But, as you say, those
pictures! those captions!

What is the comic picture-postcard but the Society
Gossip medium of the masses? If the Earl and Countess
of Bogland may have their departure to their country seat
from Elysia Square paragraphed in the higher Press, why

should not the Smiths of Holloway and the Browns of Balham inform their publics of their arrival in Sidesea. They do so inform them, and that with an *élan* all their own.   Sidesea harbour is papered with their court stationery.   A virgin card on my desk prompts the description. It pictures a middle-aged couple who have turned out on the parade—she in bland stiffness, he in juicy abandon— both lilting in their holiday best—she parasolled, he puffing a cigar with the label to vouch for it—and both living up to, nay, above, the heavy-type legend:—

They all think we're the Duke and Duchess of the place.

"This place" is Sidesea, wherever its pavilions may rule the waves.

You remember that when Mr. and Mrs. Joseph Tuggs, who might have been the models for these figures, suddenly came into twenty thousand pounds, the family—father, mother, son, and daughter—decreed an immediate departure from town.   Not for another day would they waste their superiority on their chandlery shop in a Southwark labyrinth.   "We must leave town immediately," said Mr. Simon Tuggs, who there and then vowed to sign himself "Cymon" in future.   Everyone agreed, but whither? Gravesend was "low," Margate was "all *tradespeople*," Brighton coaches were dangerous.   "'*Ramsgate*,' ejaculated Mr. Cymon thoughtfully.   To be sure; how stupid they must have been, not to have thought of that before. Ramsgate was just the place of all others."

Behold them in the Ramsgate "library."

The library was crowded.   There were the same ladies, and the same gentlemen, who had been on the sands in the morning, and on the pier the day before. There were young ladies, in maroon-coloured gowns and black velvet bracelets, dispensing fancy articles in the shop, and presiding over games of chance in the concert-room.　There were marriageable daughters, and marriage-making mammas, gaming and promenading, and turning over music, and flirting.　There were some male beaux doing the sentimental in whispers, and others doing the ferocious in moustache.　There were Mrs. Tuggs in amber, Miss Tuggs in sky-blue, Mrs. Captain Waters in pink.　There was Captain Waters in a braided surtout; there was Mr. Cymon Tuggs in pumps and a gilt waist-coat; there was Mr. Joseph Tuggs in a blue coat and a shirt frill.

There were all these people and things, but no picture-postcards.　To-day the Royal Harbour may be said to be papered with them.　Nor were the Tuggses handed pink tickets informing them that their photographs had been taken and could be had to-morrow on application.　To-day snap-photographs are to the Sidesea promenaders what the illustrated papers are to the various Smart Sets.　In both mediums the spectators, not the spectacle, are all important. I looked the other day into a shop window wholly filled with local "Coronation Snap Shots."　The camera men had known better than to focus the processions from the crowd; they had snapped the crowd from the processions. And they had their reward.

You notice, however, that in the Tuggs Period the seaside was already a market for "fancy articles."　In Sidesea to-day the visible supply of these is so prodigious that the demand seems invisible by comparison.　Strolling past these glittering bazaars I have often remembered the dry remark of Socrates in the Athenian market-place: "How many things there are in the world of which Socrates has no need."　I should like to be present when a London house-wife is buying a tea-pot moulded to look like a cottage with door and windows, and a chimney-stack by which to lift the lid; a butter dish with a cow for its handle; a

shining majolica jug with a duck's head and bill for spout;
a cruet in the shape of a railway engine; a crumb-brush
operating like a rolling street-cleaner. In London the
excited purchaser would hardly look at the things. But
here even pots and pans "suffer a sea-change into something new and strange"; and the words "A Present from
Sidesea" almost sanctify an ash-tray which would be
scorned as a present from Brixton or Ealing.

The truth is, of course, that the bazaar hunters have
themselves undergone a sea change. They have left their
year-long habits and standards behind them and need to
fill a vacuum. They have jilted sameness to fall in love
with otherness. Their home tastes are superior to those
they now indulge, and their acquisitive faculties have been
oiled. It is a rather brainless business, but there is no
harm in it. The Vicar of Wakefield's family soon recovered
from the disastrous visit of Moses to the fair where he
was to get the best price for the family's old horse. He
was perhaps overdressed for the occasion. His coat, made
of the kind of cloth known as thunder and lightning, and
his gosling green waistcoat, may have taken him a little
too much out of his normal self. True, he sold the horse
for three pounds five shillings and twopence, a sum which
would have satisfied his fond parents and sisters, but with
the money in his pocket he had unfortunately become a
dealer himself with an eye to a "dead bargain," with the
result that he brought home, not the cash, but a gross of
green spectacles, with silver rims and shagreen cases.
And as the Vicar instantly said, the rims were not silver,
adding with resignation, "Though they be copper, we will
keep them by us, as copper spectacles, you know, are
better than nothing."

To its natives Sidesea is a town, to its visitors a caravan-
serai. An old inhabitant used to say to me that he wished
the Season over so that he could meet his friends. To

N

Goethe a watering-place was an emblem of life. To Ecker-
mann he said:—

> When I look back to the earlier and middle periods
> of my life, and now in my old age think how few are
> left of those who were young with me, I think of a
> summer residence at a bathing-place. When you arrive,
> you make friends of those who have already been there
> for some time, and who leave in a few weeks. The loss
> is painful. Then you turn to the second generation,
> with which you live a good while, and become most
> intimate. But this goes also, and leaves us alone with
> the third, which comes just when we are going away,
> and with which we have really nothing to do.

To the average brief visitor the seaside responds to
whatever in him responds to the *Dulce est desipere in loco* of
Horace, to the "Do what thou wilt" of Rabelais, to the
"Many a green isle needs must be . . ." of Shelley, and
even to that now-and-then escape from the "diocese of the
strict conscience" for which Elia confessed a harmless
desire. But this is not to doubt that the Sea itself is a
minister to hurt minds. Its morning and evening moods
are like the beginning and ending of an anthem. In the
long middle hours of the day I forget it; give me then the
inland fields and copses, if work permits. But I know of
nothing in Nature so good for the inward man as the hour
when the great waters whiten under the dusk, or when far
out in the west they can be seen moving with unheard
whispers, unmindful of Man, and his wars and trinkets.

[*May* 28, 1937.]

THE HIGHER BACK-CHAT

THE recent altercation betwen Herr Hitler and Mr. Churchill was sharp enough to remind one that invective and calling names in high places are not extinct. Perhaps this is well. The erupting volcano forestalls many earthquakes. Probably David's enemy was safer when David prayed: "Let Satan stand at his right hand. Let his days be few, and let another take his office. Let his children be continually vagabonds, and beg. Let the extortioner catch all that he hath, and let the strangers spoil his labour." I am not quoting the whole imprecation. It may be that the worst enemies of Cromwell were shocked into reflection when the Anabaptists described him, in an address to Charles II, as "that grand impostor, that loathsome hypocrite, that detestable traitor, that prodigy of nature, that approbrium of mankind, that landscape of iniquity, that sink of sin, and that compendium of baseness, who now calls himself our Protector." This fulmination is quoted by Clarendon in his *History of the Rebellion*, and there is more of it.

The best specimens of invective have long become literary show pieces. In his volume, *Present Discontents*, Dr. Inge has an essay on the subject in which he describes as a "gem" the malediction pronounced hardly more than twenty years ago by the Orthodox Eastern Church, on Venizelos. It culminated in this passage:—

Wherefore against the traitor Venizelos we have invoked the following injuries: The ulcers of Job, the whale of Jonah, the leprosy of Naaman, the bite of death, the shuddering of the dying, the thunderbolt of hell, and the malediction of God and man. And we call for the same injuries on those who at the forthcoming elections shall vote for Venizelos, and further pray for their herds to wither, and for them to become deaf and blind.

It is curious, too, how these violent though short-lived emotions bring out a certain confused eloquence in people whose ordinary speech is commonplace. I remember an old lady of some position but of small education telling me in high dudgeon that someone had charged her with untruthfulness. She appealed to me heatedly: "*Me* say what ain't true? *Me* tell a lie?—Not while there's cattle on a thousand hills!"

The truth is that personal abuse is more apt to amuse the listener than to hurt the victim. Can anyone *not* laugh at Swinburne's vain attempt to crush Emerson? He had read in an American paper some abusive remarks on his own poetry attributed to Emerson, rightly or wrongly. Thereupon he wrote to Emerson tactfully, but searchingly, that he was convinced that Emerson could not have been guilty of such an attack on himself. Emerson did not reply, and Swinburne drew his own conclusions. The sequel is told by Mr. Hugh Kingsmill in his entertaining *Anthology of Invective and Abuse* as follows:—

Some months later, in February, 1874, as Swinburne and Gosse were sitting together in St. James's Park, Gosse asked Swinburne if he had ever received an answer from Emerson.

"I did NOT!" Swinburne replied.

"You will take no more notice, I suppose?"

"I have just taken exactly such notice as a gentleman in my position was bound to take. I have written him another letter."

"I hope your language was quite moderate."

"Perfectly moderate! I merely informed him, in language of the strictest reserve, that he was a gap-toothed and hoary-headed baboon who—first lifted into notice on the shoulder of Carlyle—now spits and splutters from a filthier platform of his own finding and fouling.   That is all I've said."

One can see Emerson putting this letter quietly on the fire in his Concord study.

Carlyle's invective was highly personal both to his victims and to himself; his jibes are self-revelations.   Here are some of his dicta:—

On MACAULAY: "At bottom, this Macaulay is but a poor creature, with his dictionary literature and erudition, his saloon arrogance. He has no vision in him."

On JOHN KEBLE, author of *The Christian Year*: "A little ape."

On LEIGH HUNT: "Dwarfed and dislocated into the merest imbecility."

On SHELLEY: "Poor soul, he has always seemed to me an extremely weak creature; a poor, thin, spasmodic, hectic, shrill and pallid being."

On GLADSTONE: "Gladstone appears to me one of the contemptiblest men I ever looked on. A poor Ritualist; almost spectral kind of phantasm of a man— nothing in him but forms and ceremonies and outside wrappages; incapable of seeing veritably any fact what- ever, but seeing, crediting, and laying to heart the mere clothes of the fact, and fancying that all the rest does not exist. Let him fight his own battle, in the name of Beelzebub the god of Ekron, who seems to be his God. Poor phantasm!"

On HERBERT SPENCER: "The most unending ass in Christendom."

Each of these portraitures is in part a self portrait of Carlyle himself.   But was it for this that in boyhood and youth I deified Gladstone?   For this that my young eyes gloated on him as he talked to John Bright on the Treasury Bench, and then, leaping like an old tiger to the table, answered the tearing taunts of "Randy"? For this that I fitted my boyish footsteps into his on the pavement of Abingdon Street? For this that his Hawarden postcards to my father about Home Rule were propped on a sycamore-wood bracket that I had fret-worked for their display on our sideboard? So it seems, but the corresponding fact is that I have for years inclined to think of Carlyle himself as more a phantasm than the prophet whose words I then mouthed and worshipped. *Eheu fugaces* . . . I forget at what date it was that Disraeli made his premature attempt to debunk the Grand Old Man as "a sophistical rhetorician inebriated with the exuberance of his own verbosity, and gifted with an egotistical imagination that can at all times command an interminable and inconsistent series of arguments to malign an opponent and glorify himself." Nor does it matter: they were both great servants of England and it would be worth while to hear what each of them is saying about us now.

In the Middle Ages and down to the time of Shakespeare personal abuse between scholars and doctrinaires was carried to incredible lengths. Luther described Henry VIII as "this rotten worm of the earth." Calvin, too, explored the animal creation for beasts and reptiles to whom he could liken his adversaries. He described one of them as "an ape; a great ass who is distinguished from other asses by wearing a hat; an ass with two feet; a monster composed of part of an ape and wild ass; a villain who merits hanging on the first tree we find." Yet he would claim that his language was too forbearing.

It was in the Restoration and Queen Anne periods that literary abuse became refined into satire and the cudgel less used than the rapier. The lampoon came into being in the transitional period. It has been defined as "a virulent satire either in prose or verse"; the idea of injustice and unscrupulousness seems to be essential to its definition.

Tom Brown, who wrote in one of his milder moments the
famous epigram, "I do not love thee, Dr. Fell . . ." was
king of the lampooners.   His attack on his brother versifier,
famous in his day for his *Pills to Purge Melancholy*,
began:—

> Thou cur, half French, half English breed,
> Thou mongrel of Parnassus!

After a life full of back-biting and dissipation Tom found
his last rest in the cloister of Westminster Abbey.   When
a schoolboy, making a start in English Literature, the word
"lampoon" appealed to my own puppish ferocity.   It did
also to B——'s and we fell to writing lampoons on each
other in scarifying verse to be read aloud in retired corners.
"Thou mongrel of Parnassus!" was the very vein we
worked.   Each addressed the other as the lowest of Grub
Street ink-spatterers and dullards, until our vocabulary
gave out—which it did soon enough.

The first great invector to dispense with name-calling
was Dryden.   He crushed his victims with slow, unpausing
dignity.   Richard Flecknoe as the Monarch—

> without dispute
> Through all the realms of Nonsense absolute,

is worn out and wishful to appoint his successor.

> And pond'ring which of all his sons was fit
> To reign, and wage immortal war with Wit,
> Cried, 'tis resolved; for Nature pleads that he
> Should only rule, who most resembles me:
> Shadwell alone my perfect image bears,
> Mature in dullness from his tender years;
> Shadwell alone of all my sons is he
> Who stands confirm'd in full stupidity.
> The rest to some faint meaning make pretence,
> But Shadwell never deviates into sense.

The last line has been a joy to me for more than half my life. Its justice is another matter, and can be assessed by the fact that the poet who never "deviated into sense," succeeded Dryden himself in the Laureateship.

It has been reserved for Mr. Bernard Shaw to estimate Shakespeare's genius in terms of his own, to throw the idol from his pedestal and clamber up it himself. He has never, I think, retracted these words:—

There are moments when one asks despairingly why our stage should ever have been cursed with this immortal "pilferer" of other men's stories and ideas, with his monstrous rhetorical fustian, his unbearable platitudes, his pretentious reduction of the subtlest problems of life to commonplaces against which a Polytechnic debating club would revolt, his incredible unsuggestiveness . . . With the single exception of Homer, there is no eminent writer, not even Sir Walter Scott, whom I can despise so entirely as I despise Shakespeare when I measure my mind against his. The intensity of my impatience with him occasionally reaches such a pitch that it would positively be a relief to me to dig him up and throw stones at him, knowing as I do how incapable he and his worshippers are of understanding any less form of indignity. [*Drums without.*]

[*November* 18, 1938.]

MEET WILKINSON

A STRANGE thing has happened in Erith. The Rev. J. W. Wilkinson, the newly elected Mayor of that pleasant Thames-side town, has refused to allow an Erith street to be named after him. With equal humility and courage he explains his position. "My name," he laments, "savours too much of a butler or other family servant. I dislike my name and always have disliked it—so much so that it has long been a practice of mine to sign my Christian names in full, writing John Wells Wilkinson to get a balance to my unfortunate surname.

"I consider it would be most unfair to inflict my name on any street."

It is painful to think of a man of position living on bad terms with his shadow or his surname. Of course there are unfortunate surnames, and this is no matter for surprise seeing that a vast number of surnames were originally nicknames lightly bestowed for identification purposes with a ruthless eye for personal traits or habits, physique, dress, occupation, locality, and virtues and vices—without consultation with the person most concerned. Descriptive names like Shakespear, Standfast, Golightly, and Drink-water were genial or mildly satirical, but, as Mr. Weekley points out in his excellent study, *Surnames*, many mediæval names of this type are of "quite unquotable coarseness and point either to the great brutality or great naïveté of our ancestors." A character in one of Ben Jonson's comedies declares, "Indeed, there is a woundy luck in names, sirs"; but the classic dictum on the subject is Mr. Shandy's opinion that there was a strange kind of magic bias which good or bad names, as he called them, irresistibly impressed on our character or conduct. "How many Cæsars and Pompeys," he would say, "by mere inspiration

of their names, have been made worthy of them! And
how many are there who might have done exceeding well
in the world, had not their characters and spirits been
totally depressed and Nicodemus'd into nothing." The
good Mayor of Erith beats his breast under a persuasion
that a man can be Wilkinson'd into nothing. I will deal
with his case presently.

This subtle influence of personal names on their owners,
and on those with whom they come in contact, has been
perceived since names were borne by the children of men.
But it can exalt as well as depress. "A gentleman," says
Montaigne, "one of my neighbours, who was always
preferring the excellency of preceding times in comparison
with this present age of ours, did not forget to magnify
the lofty and magnificent sound of the gentlemen's names
of those days: Don Grumedan, Quadregan, Angesilan,
etc., which but to hear named he perceived to be men of
another stamp than Peter, Giles, or Michael." In Spain a
fine name goes farther than anywhere else. Cervantes
poured gentle ridicule on this trait when he made Don
Quixote transform the name of his adored Tolosa, the
daughter of a Toledo cobbler, into a much bigger mouthful.
And Spanish wit follows suit in the story of a proud
hidalgo who arrived alone and hungry at a French village,
in which there was but a single inn. It had gone midnight
and he knocked at the door many minutes before he roused
anyone. At last the landlord put his head out of an upper
window, and cried: "Who's there?" The traveller replied:
"Don Juan, Pedro, Hermandez, Rodriguez, Alvarez de
Villanova, Count de Malafora, Cavallero de Santiago
d'Alcantara." "Mercy on us!" said the host, as he banged
the window down, "I have only two spare beds, and you
expect lodging for twenty men!" It is said that a Spanish
Ambassador to England was not a little perturbed when
Queen Elizabeth directed that he should be housed by a

wealthy citizen named John Cuts. "He imagined that a man bearing a monosyllabic name could never have performed anything great or honourable, but when he found that honest John Cuts displayed a hospitality which had nothing monosyllabic in it, he groaned only at the utterance of his host's name." Englishmen care less for the name, more for the man. "John Cuts" was as acceptable then as "John Keats" is now.

A well-sounding name is a good thing so far as it goes; a man may well take it into consideration when choosing his parents. But if he distinguishes himself, history will record his name in letters of gold, even if it should be Noggs. The poets, however, will try it on the tuning-fork first. Brass and marble alone might have perpetuated the loss of the *Royal George* if Kempenfeldt's name had not appealed to Cowper's ear, and posterity might never have glowed at the line, "And Freedom shrieked when Kosciusko fell," if the deliverer of Poland had borne a name a little less pronounceable, or even shorter by a syllable. Undoubtedly the harshness of many modern names excludes them from poetic honours in a way that is to be regretted. What modern lyrist dare spangle his verse, as did Horace, with the names of his personal friends? A Pompeius Varus, a Pollio, or a Licinius Murena, had but to be civil to Horace for a chance to "share the triumph and partake the gale" of his renown.

These blind bargains have little to do with the oldest form of surname, the simple patronymic. Johnson is for ever the son of John, Peterson of Peter, and Wilkinson of Will, Wilkie, or Wilks. Such names still, I suppose, outnumber any other type. The list of private residents in the current Post Office Directory includes more than eighty Wilkinsons, of whom, by the way, 10 per cent bear titles of one kind or another. In the *Dictionary of National Biography* the names of eight Wilkinsons who have been eminent in theology, science, engineering, geology, commerce, etc., are perpetuated: among them that of George Howard Wilkinson, successively Bishop of Truro and St. Andrew's, and the virtual organizer of the nineteenth-century Truro Cathedral. The cry, "We have no Wilkinsons to-day" has yet to be heard in the forum.

It is true that a misadventure—I will not call it a disaster—overtook this fine old name when Wordsworth published his poem, *To the Spade of a Friend: Composed while we were Labouring together in his Pleasure Ground*, and began it with the invocation:—

SPADE! *with which* WILKINSON *hath till'd his lands.* . . .

This sudden apparition of an unknown Spade in the hands of an unknown Wilkinson was too much for the critics; too much also for Tennyson, who laughed consumedly. Yet this wraith-like Wilkinson with a spade has just been made the subject of a brightly written sketch by Miss Doris N. Dalglish in her book, *People Called Quakers*, published by the Oxford University Press (7s. 6d). His Christian name was Thomas, and he was a Quaker neighbour of the Lake Poet. He wrote prose and verse himself and stood to Wordsworth in the same close relation as his contemporary Bernard Barton did to Charles Lamb. In a later note to this poem Wordsworth wrote, as I think, somewhat clumsily: "This person was a Quaker by religious profession;—by natural constitution of mind, or shall I venture to say, *by God's grace he was something better.*" The italics are mine. I wonder what my Quaker ancestors were saying about it in 1807. However, our greatest English poet since Milton meant well. He went on to state that Wilkinson "employed his leisure hours in shaping pleasant walks by the side of his beloved river [Emont], where he also built something between a hermitage and a summer-house, attaching to it inscriptions after the manner of Shenstone at his Leasowes. He used to travel from time to time, partly from love of nature, and partly with religious friends in the service of humanity. His admiration of genius in every department did him much honour." The last sentence may express an even stronger personal feeling than the others.

But this is not all: you do not so soon deflate a Wilkinson. This Quaker gentleman used his pen with as much skill as his spade, and to him we owe indirectly one of the loveliest poems in the English language. Wandering in 1787 near Loch Lomond *he*, not Wordsworth, heard—but let him tell what he heard:—

> Passed a female who was reaping alone; she sung in Erse, as she bended over her sickle; the sweetest human voice I ever heard: her strains were tenderly melancholy, and felt delicious long after they were heard no more.

At that time Wordsworth was in his teens; not till twenty years later did he read that moving sentence in Wilkinson's manuscript. Then he wrote *The Solitary Reaper*. A prose sentence that would have been utterly forgotten became a poem that none can forget. It is a happy circumstance that Wilkinson's last clause became Wordsworth's last line—as he was careful to acknowledge in a note written in 1807. The first and fourth stanzas of the poem, indeed, may be said to be Wilkinson's words set to music:—

> Behold her, single in the field,
> Yon solitary Highland lass!
> Reaping and singing by herself.
> Stop here, or gently pass!
>
> . . .
>
> I listened till I had my fill,
> And, as I mounted up the hill,
> The music in my heart I bore,
> Long after it was heard no more.

But in the second and third stanzas (the jewels within the frame) the voice is the poet's alone, his alone the spell:—

> No nightingale did ever chant
> So sweetly to reposing bands
> Of travellers in some shady haunt,
> Among Arabian sands;
> No sweeter voice was ever heard
> In spring-time from a cuckoo-bird
> Breaking the silence of the seas
> Among the farthest Hebrides.
>
> Will no one tell me what she sings?
> Perhaps the plaintive numbers flow
> For old, unhappy, far-off things,
> And battles long ago:
> Or is it some more humble lay,
> Familiar matter of to-day?
> Some natural sorrow, loss, or pain,
> That has been, and may be again!

Whatever the maiden sang, I am confident it was not the Dirge of the Wilkinsons.

P.S.—It may interest the Rev. Mayor of Erith to know that there is a Wilkinson Street not far from Lambeth Palace.

[*December* 30, 1938.]

HAVE YOU A PHOBIA?

IT is not often that one is asked for aid in dictionary English by a schoolmaster. But my friend S. P. made this demand on me a fortnight ago, and the word I undertook to find for him has given me a chase. Even the *Oxford English Dictionary* does not contain it. It was the word that means the fear of high places, or of looking down from a height. To save face I suggested that it must be one of the *phobia* words, like claustrophobia (fear of confined spaces), agoraphobia (fear of wide spaces), and hydrophobia (fear of water). My friend expressed polite dissatisfaction and gave me no peace till I found—the word.

I wanted to find it and, in the end, wrote to a younger friend who I knew was studying for a degree in Psychology and was likely to have access to a medico-psychological library. In quick and cordial answer came a list of these "phobias" such as I could not have compiled without great trouble, if at all. I am not aware that such a list has appeared in any non-technical journal. But the word? Almost everyone has feared to look down from a height, if it be from Shakespeare's Dover cliff (as in *King Lear*) or from the top of a house ladder. Well, "the Greeks had a word" or, if not, we have etymologically given them credit for it. It is ACROPHOBIA, from *akros*, meaning highest, topmost, extreme, and *phobia*, fear or horror. The term belongs, of course, to psychology and is not often heard among climbers of Beachy Head or the London Monument.

Some of these "phobia" words are well known, others hardly at all, and some—like hydrophobia, hematophobia, and toxophobia—explain themselves at sight. Here is my list to hand:—

Fear of:

high places (looking down) ..	.. ACROPHOBIA
wide spaces	.. AGORAPHOBIA
pain	.. ALGOPHOBIA
thunder and lightning ..	.. ASTROPHOBIA
confined spaces	.. CLAUSTROPHOBIA
excreta, dung	.. COPROPHOBIA
sight of blood	.. HEMATOPHOBIA
water	.. HYDROPHOBIA
speaking, attempting to speak	.. LALOPHOBIA
dirt	.. RUPOPHOBIA
dead bodies	.. NECROPHOBIA
darkness, night	.. NYCTOPHOBIA
disease	.. PATHOPHOBIA
sinning	.. PECCATOPHOBIA
speaking aloud	.. PHONOPHOBIA
light	.. PHOTOPHOBIA
eating, repugnance to food ..	.. SITOPHOBIA
premature burial	.. TAPHOPHOBIA
death	.. THANATOPHOBIA

All or nearly all these words may be regarded as coinages by psychologists, and the inclusion of some of them in the best dictionaries is still discretionary and uncertain.

"Phobia," as a separate word meaning fear, hatred, or aversion, is now an established usage and, as might be expected, has been put to semi-humorous use either alone or in hybrid compounds. Thus Anna Seward (when her revered Dr. Johnson was safely in his grave) could write of a certain man: "He is a very laconic personage, and has upon him the penphobia." Twenty years later Southey wrote of a woman acquaintance: "She laboured under a perpetual dustophobia, and a comical disease it was." Coleridge could confess, "I have a perfect phobia of inns and coffee-houses." In the 'eighties, if no earlier, such terms as Germanophobia, Francophobia, and Russophobia got into the papers and were followed by Anglophobia and even Anglophobiac. Photophobia, by the way, has nothing to do with the fear of being photographed, though in that sense it might now be useful. It is properly derived from the Greek *phōs*, and signifies the fear of light.

If it be asked why these long and ultra-classical terms are thought necessary to the naming of quite common experiences the answer is that science, philosophy, medicine, and art need vocabularies of their own. The things they deal with must be isolated, and be discussed in the cool blood of research, and new words are required for new discoveries. I might—probably would—chaff a psychologist on his use of the word peccatophobia, but he would probably defend it on the ground that in a psychological view it would be inconvenient and perhaps misleading to evoke the full suggestions of the word "sin." Similarly, if you have occasion to refer to the most familiar of eye troubles it is one thing to call it squinting and another to call it strabismus; they mean the same thing but in quite different situations. The inner meanings of these words must be sought, not in dictionaries, but in the published conclusions of medical psychologists. There is probably no one who does not hide a phobia. I confess to one; it is called *phobophobia*.

[*March* 10, 1939.]

o

IS ANYTHING NEW?

I START this letter in the dim light of an air-raid shelter under a chapel in the Isle of Thanet. About fifty people sit around, silent for the most part but unperturbed. The stairs down to this roomy cellar are of stone, the floor is asphalt and the walls lime-washed brick. A single electric bulb sheds twilight on what, in its effect on the eye, is a cave. Nothing new in *that*. Lot lived in a cave. The field for which Abraham paid four hundred shekels of silver is described almost in the language of a modern estate agent as situate in Machpelah with a cave as one of its amenities and trees bordering it round about. Five kings of the Amorites took shelter in a cave on the day when, at Joshua's bidding, the sun stood still in Gibeon. Obadiah, careful of ventilation, hid a hundred prophets "by fifty" in a cave. In all ages caves have been used as refuges, as homes for the living, and as long homes for the dead. Man is still a Troglodyte at need, so true is it that "the thing that hath been shall be . . . and there is nothing new under the sun."

The Germans have a proverb, "Nothing is so new as what has been long forgotten." I see that German shock troops in the present war are to be provided with vests of armour to protect them against machine-gun fire. Armour is not forgotten, but it is still mostly remembered in museums; will it now return to the wars? The gas-mask and the "tin hat" have led the way. One recalls Captain Gronow's vivid description of Kellermann's cavalry charging our squares at Waterloo while the bullets could be heard rattling like hail on their cuirasses. But war has no necessary connection with my theme. Seneca was not thinking of it when he asked: "What can happen that is new?" Indeed, what *can*? Can the oak produce anything but wood, leaves, and acorns? Very little reflection is needed to see that nothing *absolutely* new can come into human life. If it could—and did—it would have no relation to man: we should not so much as perceive it.

We talk of invention and originality, but neither truly exists. Man invents by instalments and originates by inspired copying. It is convenient and generous to honour a man as the inventor of something that has bene-fited the race, but in truth that thing has come from the brain of the race itself. Even in the popular sense nothing is thought of as new for very long. Said Lucretius, that sombre looker-on:—

> There's naught
> So great, so wonderful, when first 'tis seen
> But men will later cease to marvel at it.

Even small things, the gadgets of life, which we suppose to have been thrown up for the first time in our own age have, many of them, been used and forgotten. Forty years ago the taxi-meter was new to London. Very few were aware that it could be found in the lumber-rooms of China. When Milton was picturing

> the barren plains
> Of Sericana, where Chineses drive
> With sails and wind their cany waggons light

those same waggons had long been fitted with an apparatus whereby the distances they covered were indicated in the automatic beating of a drum. Our forbears could suck eggs without our help.

The dirigible airship bears the name of its "inventor," Count Zeppelin. Well, a century and a half ago something very like a Zeppelin performed its feats in the north of England—to be exact, at Wooler in Northumberland.

This was in 1790. Sir Walter Scott was at Wooler in the following year and it is a pity that he did not witness these flights. Instead, he drank the goats' whey for which Wooler was famous and turned his horse and mind to the battlefields of Flodden, Otterburn, and Chevy Chase. He mentions "trouts half a yard in length." It was in the image of a trout that the Wooler flying machine had breasted the moorland air. A local man wrote of it in a letter:—

> Some time back a gentleman, Mr. Asgill, at Byle Common, near Wooler, conceived it might be possible to conduct an air balloon in any direction, but the possibility of doing it by means of sails he some time since gave up; he next attempted to do it by means of wings, but this also failed.
>
> He then, by conceiving the air as a fluid, and remarking the method of fish swimming against a current of water, which he obtained for that purpose, has now constructed one exactly in the form of a fish, in which I yesterday saw him ascend, himself being situated in the centre of gravity: his internal machinery, which gives motion to the wings and sails, and likewise the power of removing himself to give different attitudes to the fish, is by me considered as the most ingenious piece of machinery I ever saw. . . . To see the enormous monster stretch along the air, lash his tail, skim in different directions, with all the appearance of nature, was truly admirable, and I think will be considered as the finest exhibition in the world.

Here was a flying machine that anticipated our boasted "conquest of the air." It flew over old battlefields at a height equal to that of St. Paul's Cathedral and excelled the airships of to-day in the graceful art of lashing its tail.

Telegraphy, as we know it, came in with the accession of Queen Victoria. But the *idea* of it was talked and written about in the reign of Charles I. The agent was

to be a magnetic needle turning to letters of the alphabet
and thus spelling out a message. In 1636 these lines on
the subject appeared in *Hakewell's Apology*, published at
Oxford in that year:—

> Thy friend that dwells far off, O strange! doth plainly see
> The steel to stir, though it by no man stirréd be,
> Running now here, now there: He conscious of the plot.
> As the steel guides, pursues, and reads from note to note,
> Then gathering into words those notes he clearly sees
> What's needful to be done. . . .

You may say, truly enough, that this dream was not fulfilled until two hundred years had passed. But what of
it? My point is that during that long interval, if it can
be called long, the *idea* of the electric telegraph was in the
mind of man. When it became an actuality it was already
old, for the very conception of it I have just quoted is
obviously the fruit of other and earlier thinking. Nor
can you abash me with the question: "But what about the
Telephone?" At the risk of ridicule I will declare my
belief, or at least my irrevocable surmise, that the greatest
seer and connoisseur of progress is the Poet. Of all
observers he is nearest to the hidden motions of man's
spirit. He knows more than he knows he knows; he has
divination. When the philosopher and the man of science
appear he has *been and gone*. Talk to me of Edison and the
Telephone and I think of Milton's

> aery tongues that SYLLABLE MEN'S NAMES
> On sands, and shores, and desert wildernesses.

There is the true wonder of the telephone—the word
before the thing. If, next, you challenge me to show
that Television has ever been a poet's dream I refer you to
Mr. Thomas Burke's richly discursive *Living in Bloomsbury*.
In a few pages devoted to strange anticipations he quotes

these lines from an acknowledged poet, the Countess of Winchelsea, who died more than two hundred years ago. They occur in a poem on letter-writing:—

> Oh might I live to see an art arise,
> As this to thoughts, indulgent to the eyes;
> That the dark powers of distance could subdue,
> And make me see as well as talk to you.

One more example: X-rays. What do you think of the following passage contributed to *Notes and Queries* by Mr. S. Wheeler, August 20th, 1898?

In the *Tarikhu-s Sind*, by Mir Muhammad M'asum, written A.D. 1600, there is an account of the application of the X-rays to surgical purposes. Wandering about the country near Ghuzni, an exiled prince meets a man carrying "*hukka* tubes." He is astonished to find that the man's interior economy is visible as long as the *hukka* tubes are carried on his head. He buys the tubes and takes them to Ghuzni. The king of that place is ill, having inadvertently swallowed two small water-snakes. By placing the bundle of *hukka* stems on the patient's head the exiled prince ascertains the location of the snakes, and after that their removal is a simple matter. A translation of the passage from the original Persian may be found in Elliot's *History of India by its Own Historians*.

When this was written Shakespeare was at the height of his powers, and to him let the last word be given in the words he puts into the mouth of Ulysses:—

> One touch of nature makes the whole world kin,
> That all with one consent praise new-born gawds,
> Though they are made and moulded of things past,
> And give to dust that is a little gilt
> More laud than gilt o'er-dusted.

[October 27, 1939.]

CITY CLERK'S SOLILOQUY

Waitress, my usual *café noir*,
  My usual cigarette;
Let business sleep, this hour I keep
  To brood and to forget.
I ask not that the day remit
  Its tax on bone or brow;
I ask one thing—that each day bring
  The calm I capture now.

Still let me seek at half-past one,
  This subterranean room,
Where dwells the shade that should pervade
  A temporary tomb;
A region changeless and serene,
  Where smoke for ever curls
And the same men are pleased again
  By the same smiling girls.

A fragrance haunts the café stair,
  A thrice familiar din,
And the red stars of strong cigars
  Invite the stranger in;
And City faces, sternly set,
  Round marble tables gleam,
Where to and fro the domino
  Is moving in a dream.

Enjoy the day, old Horace sang,
  Enjoy the hour say I,
And wisely sup the Arab's cup
  Ere life's be running dry.
Possess your soul, if only here,
  Where smoke for ever curls,
And the same men are pleased again
  By the same smiling girls.

[November 14, 1902.]

MARGARINE IN WAR AND PEACE*

WITH all Europe rocking, the question whether the "g" in margarine should be pronounced hard or soft becomes momentous. At any rate M. M. (Eastbourne), a woman reader, writes: "We have had *such* a discussion at lunch to-day about this. I think *hard*, but said I should write and ask you." Though I do not happen to consume margarine I use the *soft* "g," which I imagine spreads better on toast. There is a know-all-about-it story that the man who first put margarine on the market named it after his wife or daughter, Margaret, and from this it is argued that the "g" should be hard. Even if the story is true I do not think it imposes this pronunciation on public usage.

Margarine was a well-known substance before it became a breakfast-table delicacy. The O.E.D. cites a United States patent specification so far back as 1875 in which it was stated: "Margarine is no novelty; it was brought out two or three years ago in Paris." In 1887 there was a big fight in the House of Lords about claims to use the terms, Margarine and Butterine. A year later *The Times* recorded that "after adopting successively the names of oleo-margarine, butterine, and margarine, Parliament finally, after several struggles, resolved on the last." A week or two later the same newspaper announced: "Margarine, as we formally record this morning, has begun its actual legislative existence."

Its literary existence was not long delayed, for in 1891 that fine etcher, Sir Francis Seymour Haden, could describe

---

* This is one of the series of articles in *John o' London's Weekly* in which Wilfred Whitten regularly discussed points of English usage. They appeared under the general headline *Passing Remarks*, and were signed "Jackdaw." I have chosen this particular article for inclusion here because of its typicalness rather than the significance of its subject matter.—F.W.

a certain art production as "one of those things which I fear I must call a 'margarine' substitute for etching." The noun became a verb in *Punch*, in the year of the Armistice, in the sentence, "She knows which side her bread's margarined."

But what about that " g "? The etymology of "margarine," taken alone, undoubtedly favours the hard pronunciation preferred by M. M.—the word being derived from margaric acid, a natural ingredient of certain animal and vegetable oils, found in mutton suet, hog's head, etc. The name margarine was in fact chosen because of a resemblance in tint to the pearl (Latin, *margarita*) and therefore to Margaret. But the popular pronunciation is "mar*j*arine," as is conceded without censure by the Oxford English Dictionary, Wyld's Universal, and Chambers's. And since margarine is now an everyday household commodity I am of opinion that its *folk* pronunciation has claims that override those advanced by scholars and that it will prevail. When we adopt a word from the Latin or Greek we make it our own and—short of any ridiculous effect—we have the right to make it as English as we please. This may not be the law, but it is the prophets.

*   *   *   *   *

Another question in pronunciation—but one that admits of a decisive answer—comes from F. W. P. (Newport, Mon.), who writes:

> I have always pronounced "suit" to rhyme with "cute" and "Susan" with the first syllable to rhyme with "due." My daughters insist that I must pronounce the "su" as "soo"—"Soosan." Will you kindly express an opinion?

In *suit* both values may be given to the *u* sound; it is a matter of taste, though the now usual pronunciation produces a rhyme to "boot," not to "newt." But the

pronunciation of *Su* in Susan to rhyme with "few" is
something I have never heard, and I hope shall never hear.

> All in the Downs the fleet was moor'd,
>   The streamers waving in the wind,
> When black-eyed S-yew-san came aboard:
>   O! where shall I my true-love find?
> O S-yew-san, S-yews-an, lovely dear,
>   My vows shall ever true remain . . .

No, it won't do.

*   *   *   *   *

I wish an agreed answer could be found to the question
of using the prefix "Messrs." before the name of a commercial company. This recurrent dispute almost inter-
feres with my sleep, and the worst of it is that my own
answer is liable to be turned down as no answer.

Why should "Limited" preclude the courtesy use of
"Messrs."? It is merely short for "Limited Liability"
(Company): it does not dehumanize the directors or shareholders, but limits their ultimate liability to the value of
their shares. A Limited Company consists of individuals
who bleed when they are pricked and smile when they
are flattered. Why deny them the conventional courtesy
of "Messrs." on an envelope, where it simply means
"Masters," thus: "Messrs. (Masters of) The Australian
Gas Light Co., Ltd."?

My correspondent brushes away the consideration of
courtesy with the comment: "Surely to be courteous does
not demand that we perpetrate a solecism." Now a
solecism is an error in the nature of an incongruity or
faulty concord, an inconsistency. Well, our courtesy
language is riddled with solecisms. It is surely a solecism
to address a tradesman as an Esquire, yet it is done, and
expected to be done. I commit a solecism willingly when
I sign myself, as I do here, my correspondent's obedient
and humble servant, JACKDAW.

[*November* 24, 1939.]

WAR IN WAR-TIME

IT is no paradox that we are less willing to think seriously about War while we are at war than in time of peace. If advised to do so we reply with vernacular impatience—"Oh, stow it! There's a war on."

When the police station siren blows our powers of generalisation are suspended. Headlines, too, as they enlarge or diminish, blur our eye for events. We are swayed and puzzled alternately by news often deeply coloured at its source, then interrupted, censored, variously interpreted, and soon superseded. All this and a hundred personal results explain that war vertigo from which only a grim sense of humour can save us but of which in moments of candour we make no secret. Is there a sedative which is not a dope?

Perhaps there is no better way to obtain a larger and stiller outlook on the present War—unexampled in history —than by dipping into the story of wars whose throbs of heroism and pain and hope and fear come to us down the ages. These wars are summarised, their accounts are made up. It is in them that we can see War as the most gigantic and terrible expression of human energy and suffering. They help us to see Armageddon steadily, and to see it whole. For the mind of man is rested and fortified by the discovery that the glories and calamities of his time are not new.

In reading Thucydides or Herodotus we find that men felt about the wars of two to three thousand years ago just as we feel about our own; that the core of the matter was the same, and the train of events strangely like in essentials. We see that guns, shells, trenches, war in the sky, war under the sea, anæsthetics and Anderson shelters are but accidents in a business that has engaged man intermittently, yet with seeming punctuality, through the ages; and that love of liberty, race consciousness, sacrifice, greed, mercy and devilry are its abiding elements. The long advance from sword and shield to bomb and shelter has little significance: War knows progress as well as Peace.

But have the morals of War sunk? To-day our own signals and sirens give us warning of assault. In ancient times it was the enemy who gave the warning. War by stealth or "blitz" was held to be unworthy and unfair. When Lucius Marcius gained time to reorganise his army by pretending to the King of Macedon that he was ready to talk peace, the Roman Senate condemned his trick "as degenerating from the ancient practice, which they said was by valour, and not by artifice, surprises, and night encounters; neither by pretended flight, ambuscades, and deceitful treaties." I quote Montaigne who quotes Polybius. As for *blitzkrieg*, it is recorded that in the kingdom of Ternates it was the custom, before making war, to give the intended enemy exact information of its army's strength in men and armaments before striking. The ancient Florentines so far forswore all surprise that they gave a month's warning to the enemy by the continual tolling of a bell which they called the *Martinella*. To-day the cynical comment on such policy would be *O sancta simplicitas!*

On such contrasts it is useless to dwell even if they are as typical as they seem. It is more profitable to notice the resemblances between modern and ancient war where they lie deepest—in the ideals which men fought for and died to save. How strangely, even weirdly, applicable to our present struggle are the words of Pericles to the Athenians in 431 B.C. at the beginning of the long Peloponnesian War. Here are a few of them:—

Our constitution does not copy the laws of neighbouring States; rather we are a pattern to others than imitators ourselves. Its administration favours the many instead of the few; that is why it is called a democracy.

The freedom which we enjoy in our government extends also to our private life. There, far from exercising jealous surveillance over each other, we do not feel called upon to be angry with our neighbour for doing what he likes, or even to indulge in those injurious looks which cannot fail to be offensive, although this inflict no positive penalty. But all this ease in our private relations does not make us lawless as citizens.

We throw open our city to the world, and never by alien acts exclude foreigners from any opportunity of learning or observing, although the eyes of any enemy may occasionally profit by our liberality; trusting less in system and policy than to the native spirit of our citizens; while in education, where our rivals from their very cradles by a painful discipline seek after manliness, at Athens we live exactly as we please, and yet are just as ready to encounter every legitimate danger. And if with habits not of labour but of ease, and courage not of art but of nature, we are still willing to encounter danger, we have the double advantage of escaping the experience of hardships in anticipation and of facing them in the hour of need as fearlessly as those who are never free from them.

These words seem curiously familiar. For among the many charges that are brought against us by others, though quite as often by ourselves, are these: that as a people we lack discipline, that our educational system is at loose ends, and that our hospitality to foreigners is suicidal. And yet we remain persuaded that our "national genius"—at which many people are ready to scoff because it does not seem to include the labelled qualities of other nations—is still our strength. If that is so, if the character of Britons is composed of qualities which cannot be easily catalogued because they are unseen in the blood rather than exposed on the surface, if totality of character rather than advertised virtues is our shield—then we may cease to wonder that Pericles saw the Athenians so nearly as we see ourselves.

When in the first phase of the War of 1914–1918 the Kaiser scoffed at our "contemptible little army," and his own army criticised our men as better able to play games than to fight, they were repeating history. When Xerxes was invading Greece one of his spies brought him word that the Spartans, under Leonidas, were some of them doing gymnastic exercises and others combing their long hair. "'Arf a mo', Xerxes," seemed to be their mood. When Xerxes was told this he was amazed. Herodotus explains that he had no means of surmising the truth—namely that the Spartans were preparing to do or die manfully—but thought it laughable that they should be engaged in such employments. He sent and called to his presence Demaratus, the son of Ariston. When he arrived Xerxes told him all he had heard and questioned him, being anxious to understand the meaning of such extraordinary behaviour on the part of the Spartans:—

Then Demaratus said: "Earnestly do I struggle at all times to speak truth to thee, Sire; and now listen to it once more. These men have come to dispute the pass with us; and it is for this that they are now making ready. 'Tis their custom, when they are abroad to hazard their lives, to adorn their heads with care. Be assured, however, that if thou canst subdue the men who are here and the Lacedæmonians who remain in Sparta, there is no other nation in the world which will venture to lift a hand in their defence. Thou hast now to deal with the finest kingdom and town in Greece, and with the bravest men."

Then Xerxes, to whom what Demaratus said seemed altogether to surpass belief, asked further: "How is it possible for so small an army to contend with mine?"

"O King!" Demaratus answered. *"Let me be treated as a liar, if it falls not out as I say."*

The story offers a picture of free and easy espionage which suggests comic opera rather than war. Xerxes, on occasion, actually welcomed spies, regarding them as more useful than dangerous. When in his great march to the Bosphorus he lay at Sardis, three Greek spies who arrived there were caught and sentenced to instant death by his generals. But Xerxes hearing of this ordered the spies to be brought before him, when to their astonishment and the chagrin of the generals he further ordered his guards to show them round the camp and then, when they had seen all they wished, to send them back unharmed to their country. He afterwards explained his action. Had the spies been put to death, he said, the Greeks would have remained ignorant of the vastness of his army, which surpassed the common report, whereas he would have done them a very small injury by killing three spies. By the return of the spies his power would become known and the Greeks, he expected, would surrender without a battle. This reasoning was not justified by the result, but then Xerxes had miscalculated the spirit of the Greeks quite as much as they may have under-rated his forces.

Even more whimsical was Xerxes' attitude in another matter. While waiting at Abydos with his fleet he saw some corn ships passing through the Hellespont. His men wished to capture them, but Xerxes asked whither the ships were bound. The answer was: "For thy foes, master, with corn on board." To which Xerxes replied: "We, too, are bound thither, laden, among other things, with corn. What harm is it if they carry our provisions for us?"

It would be easy to multiply these parables. Nor do

the historians of these old wars, waged so differently from ours, fail to suggest the tragic enigma of it all. Take a story of Cyrus and Crœsus. The victorious Persian had his Lydian captive thrown in fetters upon a pyre, which was presently ignited. Then he relented, and ordered the flames to be extinguished. When Crœsus was safe, Cyrus asked him "who it was that persuaded him to lead an army into his country, and so to become his foe rather than continue his friend." And Crœsus replied: "What I did, O King, was to thy advantage and my own loss. If there be blame, it rests with the god of the Greeks, who encouraged me to begin the war. No one is so foolish as to prefer war to peace, in which, instead of sons burying their fathers, fathers bury their sons. But the gods willed it so." It was the speech of a war-maker in war-time.

[*January* 3, 1941.]

WHAT IS SUPERSTITION?

I ASK the question because it presented itself to me unexpectedly the other day, and is of general as well as personal interest. A man of brains once told me that he had not a single superstition in his mental make-up. I might have suggested to him that this was his superstition number one. We are all more superstitious than we are willing to admit, and although our contempt for other people's superstitions may be honest it is not always justified.

To come to the point. I had picked up a local weekly newspaper and had found in it a two-column report headed, *Youth's Suicide on Eve of Full Moon*. That roused my interest, for on the same evening I had gazed at the moon rising in copper glory above this little town. I now read the sad story of a hopeful and ought-to-have-been happy boy of seventeen who had taken his life. He had left a moving and well-written letter to his sweetheart in which he said: "I have made up my mind, dearest, to take my life. . . . The jury will most probably return a verdict of 'Suicide whilst of unsound mind,' but, believe me, I am sounder in mind now than I have been for a long time." In a boy of little more than school-leaving age this was of course proof of the mental unsettlement he repudiated. The evidence showed that he had a good home, that he was an ardent and happy lover, that he was doing well in his employment, and that he had no money or other conspicuous troubles. His mother's suggestions of cause or motive amounted to little. Her son had been somewhat upset by a bomb experience, he had recently complained that he had too little time to himself, and he did not like the place to which he had been sent in the course of his employment. He seemed to be more anxious to be married than is usual in a youth in the early stage of courtship.

In all this there was nothing more than the ordinary troubles of youth, and in his summing-up the Coroner said that the boy seemed to have taken his life for "absolutely no cause at all." On the other hand, he had written to his girl friend: "I hate life. I hate myself." His young heart knew its own bitterness. And here comes in another scrap of the mother's evidence: she said, apparently as a mere afterthought, that her boy had always seemed to be rather unsettled during the term of the full moon, but added that she had put this down to her own imagination. I was struck by this statement, and so (I found) had been the Coroner, for when the doctor concerned in the case was called he said to this witness: "You have heard what the mother has said about her son apparently being unsettled

P

when the moon was full.   Are people inclined to be more unsettled when the moon is full?"   The doctor replied: "I don't think there is any scientific basis for any theory that the phases of the moon affect human beings."   The Coroner ended this dialogue with the remark: "There is sometimes some trace of fact you cannot understand in some of these old superstitions."

The Coroner's view and the doctor's seem to be alike reasonable, though neither is conclusive.   What kind and what amount of evidence are needed to establish a "scientific basis" for an old belief, I do not know.   The belief that the full moon does sometimes affect the human mind is very old and still widely held.   This fact does not answer the doctor's scepticism, but what about ordinary observation and experience?   Some years ago I happened to fall into talk with a "mental" nurse and I took the opportunity to raise this question.   She promptly and strongly assured me that this influence of the moon was a commonplace of her experience.   When the moon was full her hands became full.   Not only so: she had found that not a few of her patients knew that they would be at their worst when the moon was full and would bespeak her special attention: "You will take care of me, won't you?"   The other day, in discussing the tragedy I have mentioned, I was told by an acquaintance that when he was a small boy he had noticed that at mysterious intervals those patients who were regularly taken for country walks were accompanied by more attendants than usual.   At last he asked the reason —to be told that this increase in supervision was regularly made at this period.   It has never, I think, been suggested that the full moon causes mental unrest but only that it aggravates any that may exist.   That, however, while it moderates the effect, seems to diffuse it more widely.

Myth, history, and literature combine to support this "superstition" of lunar influence on the mind.   What,

then, *is* superstition? The word changes in meaning—
at any rate in applicability—as knowledge grows. But
while knowledge comes superstition lingers. Is its lingering any proof that it is not still, in measure, knowledge, or
is it rather the contrary? The word superstition does not
by derivation contain the idea of falsity or delusion; it
means simply a *standing over*, with the implied notion of
awe or wonder. Much superstition was once knowledge
and may still be half-knowledge; it is too soon to throw
it as rubbish to the void. A great many practices and
prejudices have become " superstitions " because the notions
of good or ill luck have been tacked to them; the superstitious element is really an afterthought. The credulous
fail to distinguish between confirmation and coincidence.
The supposed unluckiness of the number 13 is put down to
the fact that this was the number of persons at the Last
Supper, of whom one, Judas Iscariot, soon afterwards
hanged himself. In reality the belief is much older and
therefore has a different origin.

Had the number of guests at the Last Supper been eleven,
fourteen, or some other number, that number would have
acquired the same repute as thirteen and with as little reason.
The reasonable chance that one of thirteen people taking
a meal together will pass away at no distant date is not
considered, but when this does happen the coincidence
(it is not really one) is rashly taken as proof of the belief.
Such fulfilments are no doubt sometimes startling. In
August, 1885, Sir John Millais gave a dinner in honour of
Matthew Arnold. On this occasion (we are told in his
biography) one guest made a late discovery that there
were thirteen at table and expressed some fear of the sequel.
Matthew Arnold laughed and said: "The idea is that whoever leaves the table *first* will die within a year." That
is a version of the superstition that I have not met with
elsewhere. However, Arnold went on: "So, with the

permission of the ladies, we will cheat the fates for once. I and these strong 'lads' (indicating Edgar Dawson and E. S.) will rise together, and I think our united constitutions will be able to withstand the assault of the Reaper." Only six months later Arnold died suddenly at the age of sixty-six. A few days later E. S. was found dead in his bed. Seven months after the dinner Edgar Dawson, returning from Australia, was drowned when the steamship *Quetta* sank with all hands off the coast of New Guinea. A triple fulfilment of the omen. But surely so much less a fulfilment because triple and because unprecedented. I have read somewhere that actuarial calculations have shown that, taking the world's population as a whole, one death in thirteen within one year is the proportion to be expected. Although the superstition can have had no such basis its foundation in normal truth is suggested.

Just as widespread to-day is the old belief that it is unlucky to spill salt. My friend Mr. Arthur Machen seems to share my inclination to see superstition and knowledge as the same thing in different stages or states. On this particular belief he wrote many years ago: "At present one cannot see the remotest connection between spilling the salt and misfortune; still it is possible that the connection exists, and that to our descendants it may seem the merest commonplace of the most ordinary person." I think that the popular belief merely registers and exaggerates the feeling that must have been common when the virtues of salt were understood but the supply of it meagre. This feeling may well go back to classical periods when salt was used in sacrificial rites and was esteemed as an emblem of purity. We read in *Leviticus*: "And every oblation of thy meat offering shalt thou season with salt; neither shalt thou suffer the salt of the covenant of thy God to be lacking from thy meat offering." The modern ladder superstition I would place in the same category, though much lower down; it is a warning against immediate ill-fortune, not an omen. I once saw a man painted green from head to foot when he walked under a ladder.

To return to Moon lore, science may not confirm the belief that the full moon affects some minds unfavourably, but neither, so far as I am aware, does science deny it. We stand in a unique relation to the Moon. Alone among the heavenly bodies the Moon is an offspring of our Earth. It is part of our planet still, though a migrant on leash. Its attraction is the cause of our sea and ocean tides, and through these, if not in more direct ways, it influences our planet's weather and a great many of our daily habits, fears and precautions. Its direct influence on organic life is accepted by countless tillers of the soil whether it has any "scientific basis" or not. Are the Essex mushroom growers merely deluded when they say that mushrooms wax with the waxing moon and shrink as the moon wanes? They ought to know.

The belief that the mind of man comes under lunar influence is as old as the hills. Cleopatra, we may be sure, had it in her life as she has it still in Tennyson's *Dream of Fair Women* :—

> She, flashing forth a haughty smile, began:
> "I govern'd men by change, and so I sway'd
> All moods. 'Tis long since I have seen a man.
> Once, like the Moon, I made
> The ever-shifting currents of the blood
> According to my humour ebb and flow,
> I have no men to govern in this wood:
> That makes my only woe."

Moonlight creeps and sleeps in all poetry and romance. The legend of the Man in the Moon has no "scientific" basis, but is it without a spiritual one? This might be called a compulsory superstition. Man has even professed to identify his lunar brother, calling him now Cain and now identifying him with the unhappy wight who was haled before Moses for gathering sticks upon the Sabbath day. All superstition of course, but of the kind that knowledge cannot extinguish. Superstition is a realm in which cause and effect lose much of their meaning, but not all. Once organic to knowledge and now inorganic, once logical and now mythological, once brass tacks and now fluff, "Superstition" survives. It survives because it is necessary to man and ineradicable from his consciousness.

I have not answered my own question. Nor can I think how to evade it but in feeble parody of a famous couplet:—

> You may scorn, you may smother, the tale as you will,
> But the aura of Truth will shine from it still.

[*April* 11, 1941.]

THE BEST OF LIFE

HAS it ever occurred to you that our most enduring memories are of the least memorable things? Outstanding events and crises in our lives are, of course, vividly, often too vividly, remembered, but they do not seem to revisit us of their own motion; they wait to be evoked. Whereas the memories I have in mind are become as much part of us as gold-fish of the bowl in which they dwell; now one and now another comes wantonly into view and will do so at intervals to the end; they are at home. They have no conventional importance, being mostly born of mere states of mind, impressions, sudden insights, and things seen and felt by seeming chance. We have no record of them unless—but very rarely—in a sketch, a diary, or a few attempts of verse. The great majority of such

experiences are their own historians in a language that we
can hardly now translate.

Looking the other day through an old collection of
cuttings, I found some feeble lines that I scribbled many
years ago in a small suburban garden. I had forgotten
that I possessed them except in memory. Under the title,
Calm, they ran thus:—

> A plot of grass reposing in
>   The shadow of a lime,
> A sleeping cat, a puppy's tin,
>   And half a whiff of thyme.
>
> Suburban belfries that repeat
>   Their sober invitation,
> A Sabbath footfall in the street,
>   A sense of the Creation!
>
> A heart at once subdued and free,
>   A wise and idle calm,
> And London like a breathless sea
>   Or like a breathéd psalm.

A poor thing, as you see, but a record of one of those
chance hours which come to each of us without notice
given and without our seeking, and which I here call the
best of life. They are the unearned increment of our
works and days. They come as Shelley saw them—rather
too sadly for my present purpose—among the Euganean
hills:—

> Many a green isle needs must be
> In the deep wide sea of misery,
> Or the mariner, worn and wan,
> Never thus could voyage on
> Day and night, and night and day,
> Drifting on his dreary way . . .
> O'er the unreposing wave,
> To the haven of the grave.

But he flings aside this wispish melancholy to lose himself

in his actual surroundings—"the waveless plain of Lombardy" and far-off Venice taking the sunrise while

> Column, tower, and dome and spire,
> Shine like obelisks of fire.

He sees the sapphire-tinted skies as the realm where Apollo spoke of old. Such divine leisures waylay us. Are we not all haunted by certain landscapes that come back unbidden, not as topographical facts but as vestures of the soul? Their charm is within us, and their full meaning incommunicable. "Is it not the best of life—that involuntary flash of memory upon instants of the eager past?"— George Gissing asks in one of his novels. I make an affirmative answer with no reserve.

Leaving out childhood, one of my first green isles was a big turnip field. It was in a purely agricultural country not more than a dozen miles from Oxford, and its crop was the sort of big turnips known as swedes. When autumn came we boys—few, I think, over fourteen or fifteen years—were paraded to receive old kitchen knives, and were led to the turnips, which we had to uproot, behead, and clean of loose earth before throwing them into orderly heaps. Some boys (I fancy they were farmers' sons) despised this work as beneath them; to me, coming from a black north of England town, it was a joy. One evening, when working somewhat alone, my eyes were opened to see nothing but earth and crop. Stooping and turning about, I had lost my bearings, and the world had become a field among uncharted fields in which I bent my small back and smelled the soil; all else was non-existent. Nothing familiar happened; no one spoke to me; I was original as Adam. Well, this unmemorable memory still returns, not as a mere episode but as an expansion of *ego*. In itself nothing to relate, it is interned in him who now bores you by relating it. Yet here there is a moral. It is—that of these evanescent yet haunting things the soul is greatly composed.   They are the rungs in Jacob's ladder.

It is these visions that one does not need to call up—because they come back as they list, transfigured sometimes in a light that never was on sea or land—that Gissing hails as the best of life.   Some affinity surer than taste or selection accounts for their tenancy of the inmost chambers.   And not seldom the memory takes on its significance long after the event.   Behind the central building of my second school there was an oblong paddock which we called the Little Field.   It was enclosed on three sides by the school buildings and on the fourth by a miry lane and a row of great elms.   For long I had a quite ordinary memory of this rather sunless space, into which we looked when we took our ailments to the surgery to be sorted into real and sham by the Matron.   Years later I read Tennyson's verse:—

> While now we sang old songs that peal'd
>   From knoll to knoll to knoll, where couched at ease
>   The white kine glimmer'd and the trees
> Laid their dark arms about the field.

Instantly and for ever the last line brought back the Little Field; impossible to separate the two impressions, born far apart.   Twenty-six years ago I was in Rome, new to its grandeurs.   Which of these impressed me first and most? The stars.   In London the same night-sky would have been like another; I might have glimpsed Orion or the Plough and walked on unthinkingly.   But to see the same stars shining over the city of all the Cæsars and all the Pontiffs was a thrill beyond temples and forums and prodigies of art.   Thus had Romulus and Virgil seen them. Lucretius saw them with his eyes to the ground: a street puddle of not more than an arm's length had given him "a view beneath the earth of a reach as vast as that which the high yawning maw of heaven opens out above the earth; so that you see the hordes of birds far withdrawn into the wondrous sky beneath the earth." Even he wrote nothing more simple and sublime.

Without doubt these intimations of our mortality, or immortality, are peculiar to youth and to first experiences. Wordsworth knew this when in his great Ode he addressed the Child as "the best philosopher," and said:—

> Full soon thy soul shall have her earthly freight,
> And custom lie upon thee with a weight,
> Heavy as frost, and deep almost as life

But we cannot plan or contrive these great insights; in vain we forage for them. Thus in his chapter on *The Moral of Landscape* Ruskin says that if we try to do so it is all over with our enjoyment, and that the first point of wisdom in this matter is to be content with as little novelty as possible. He goes on to suggest that a turn of a country road, with a cottage beside it, is as much as we need for refreshment. Rembrandt thought the same, as I long ago learned from his drawings and etchings of land-scape. The Netherlands were not too flat for him, or too void of rhetoric. His subjects have titles no more arresting than *Farm buildings and trees beside a lane* or *Canal and towing-path*. All are masterpieces of swift, intimate rendering of such landscapes as he had known all his life. He made such scenes Everyman's because he loved them and had first made them his own. To him they were not "subjects," but symbols of his inner life. A fine landscape painter of our own time whom I had the privilege to know slightly gave these maxims to young artists: "Your attitude towards Nature should be respectful, but at the same time confident. One should love Nature without giving up one's authority. . . . In making a sketch from Nature, you must be strung to a high pitch. If you have no enthusiasm, and lack courage, stay at home and do other work that befits your temperament." But this "enthusiasm" has nothing to do with technique, or reputation, or money. It is of the soul. We do not see a landscape only with our eyes; we see it through a mood which appoints the place in the brain on which the scene shall strike. Sir Alfred East, whose words I have quoted, said "Landscape painting is the realisation of inspired conceptions. . . . Imitation is not art." To a true artist Nature is the best of life. It was so to Amiel, who wrote in his Journal: "Every landscape is a mood." How did Constable find his subjects? He looked within himself. "The sound of water escaping from mill-dams, etc., willows, old rotten planks, slimy posts, and brickwork —I love such things. As long as I do paint I shall never cease to paint such places. Painting is with me but another word for feeling, and I associate my 'careless boyhood' with all that lies on the banks of the Stour." I have wandered along that quiet river and know its reeds and tow-paths. Not here would a painter come to heap Ossas of the picturesque on Pelions of the sublime; here are no hills or foaming cascades, no crags nodding to the moon; but willows and water-meadows, and sheets of kingcups, and 'old rotten planks' and—oneself.

For each of us the beauty of our world is where we find it, not so often where we seek it by formula or when ruled by fashion. How often we find that the best of life is not in the earthquake and not in the fire, but in some still, small voice.

[*April* 25, 1941.]

A BOOK THAT WILL LIVE

I THINK that the book before me *The Right to Live*, will be read a hundred years hence and for longer. It will be read, not as a commentary on the present World War, but as a view of the conditions which have made such a war possible.

The book is a collection of essays by the late Max Plowman, poet, essayist, and philosopher, who died a little more than two years ago at the age of fifty-seven. Charged with his deepest thoughts and feelings, it is his testament of life and death. In a wholly sympathetic introduction, Mr. John Middleton Murry describes it as "this wise and beautiful book." On its wisdom very different judgements will no doubt be passed, but hardly on its beauty, which, whether or not it is accepted as the beauty of truth, is beyond doubt the beauty of truth-seeking. It is the beauty of the truth which the world awaits and which we are now fighting to establish. The core and burden of Plowman's message lies in his conversion to Pacifism (as he understood pacifism) in 1917, when he had already served as an officer in our battles on the Somme. It was finally brought about, if not by a vision, by a visitation, and this is his account:

> I was sitting in an Army tent at Chelmsford reading Tagore on "Nationalism," considering the argument quite objectively, when suddenly I knew that I had no right to be in the Army. The conviction was immediate, and seemingly spontaneous. But it was ludicrous, absurd, impossible beyond entertainment: there I was, very definitely in the British Army. It was futile to think I had no right to be. Then it was as if a voice added: "And now you have to come out of it."

Circumstances permitted him to resign his commission, and he did.

Of course I knew and felt that from one standpoint I was only another adjectival "Conchy" letting his pals down. Socially I had on the instant become an outcast. It couldn't be helped: I had found nothing I did not wish to share, and Paul's reply to Agrippa (*Acts* xxvi. 2) was true of me. But every great decision in life has to be made in a man's soul as though it and truth existed alone in the world.

But Max Plowman's renunciation of war was less simple than that.

No "pacifist" in the common-talk sense, Plowman denounced, not the War, but the social and political conditions which had led to it. He wrote:

There is a wide difference between the will to *resist* war and the decision to *renounce* it; for he who renounces an activity judges himself, whereas he who resists an activity passes judgement on others. If I renounce war, that will very speedily involve me in the necessity to create a new social harmony, whereas if I merely resist war, no such consequence is implied.

Thus Plowman speaks his mind, not as a Pacifist or Socialist or any other *ist*, but as a man thinking about Man. He throws back the responsibility for War on the errors of Peace; asking, in effect, why in Peace we lay a deadly train of gunpowder and are shocked when it explodes as War. Why, when we are in the midst of War, do we become quite unusually interested in social justice? Is it because the one-ness of War and Peace is illuminated for us by the lightnings of tragedy?

Plowman sees war and peace as phases of the same struggle for existence; bombs and tanks as variants of capitalist rule and trade competition. So does Mr. Murry. He applauds the early Quakers as the first English war-resisters, but he points out that they saw no connection between war by the sword and war by competition for the means of life. "They became some of the finest exponents of the virtues and vices of capitalism: great industrialists, great bankers, whose word was as good as their bond." For them trade and peace were one. But he is certain that they were not hypocrites. "They were merely unaware." Plowman himself states the case more broadly:

Man inevitably defends himself against competing man, and in doing so the competition inevitably becomes intensified. Thus the primary struggle with nature is diverted from the true antagonist and becomes a competitive fight for life between man and man. Meliorated and disguised by a thousand compensating and strictly human activities, this competitive struggle for security of life goes on becoming necessarily more and more intense, until finally the ordinary means of gaining self-advantage prove insufficient to whole bodies of men, who find themselves, again inevitably, ranged against one another in the struggle for the means of life. Follows war as naturally as night follows day. War will in fact continue to be the *normal* activity of man so long as competition for the means of subsistence is regarded as a basic rule of human life.

A few years ago this would have been ignored as Socialist rant; to-day it is at least secure of attention.

It will be suggested, nevertheless, that Plowman's refusal to denounce what he renounced shows that he did not know his own mind. But in this matter the struggle between faith and fact is hard and difficult. We see this in the attitude of the Churches to war—a subject too large for discussion here. Take, instead, a personal dilemma like Plowman's, and its different solution. When Tennyson wrote (in 1854) his *Charge of the Heavy Brigade at Balaclava* he added to it an epilogue, probably now almost forgotten, which takes the form of an argument between himself and a young woman who has read his poem:

IRENE.
Not this way will you set your name
  A star among the stars.

POET.
What way?

IRENE.
You praise when you should blame
  The barbarism of wars.
A juster epoch has begun.

POET.
You wrong me, passionate little friend,
  I would that wars should cease . . .
But since our mortal shadow Ill
  To waste this earth began—
Perchance from some abuse of Will
  In worlds before the man
Involving ours—he needs must fight,
  To make true peace his own.
He needs must combat Might with Might,
  Or Might would rule alone.

These lines, written thirty years before he was born, might
well have been a comment on Max Plowman's renunciation
of War. They would have presented him with the
argument that self-preservation is the first law of life, and
that therefore Hitler's might *must* be crushed by might.

Here we have the collision between one man's sense of
reality and another man's faith in an ideal. Plowman, as
I have shown, had seen war in its reality when he renounced
it in 1918. In 1939, defining his position anew, he roundly
denied that self-preservation is the first law of life:

For it isn't. It is the first law of the unconscious
beast, and man of course inherits the instinctive traits
of the most ruthless of the animals, red in tooth and
claw. But man is conscious; and consciousness means
what it implies—understanding of process. And man
is aware of the fact that the cause of his life is the
love of one human being for another—that without

that love he would have no existence. . . . Hence it follows that the idea that each one of us ought to be self-sufficient, and that this is our principal duty, is not founded on biological fact. . . . Love, and not self-preservation, is the first law of human nature.

Here Plowman's faith seems clearer than his reasons for it. Self-preservation is not the first law of living *well*, but it is the first law of living *at all*, and this is a biological fact for both man and beast. In both the law of self-preservation operates only when danger threatens, and then it takes quick precedence of all other natural laws. True, it is waived by the martyr, but self-preservation is then seen at its noblest. Tennyson seems to have the best of it.

But Plowman sees this plea (answering the challenge, "What would you do *if* . . .?") as a mere evasion of the question, "Why War at all?" He refuses to believe that this world cancer is beyond treatment and cure:

All down the ages we see the stock of human life steadily rising in value. First cannibalism is abolished: then human sacrifice. Philosophy in the East becomes entangled with the metaphysical idea that *all* life is sacred, and religion, misinterpreting the truth, initiates the worship of animals; but the search for new value in life goes on. Slowly and reluctantly society ceases to take vengeance upon diseased and insane persons; the leper is tended, the mad are no longer stoned. Slowly the old personal gratification at the execution of murderers is disowned. . . . All these are signs of a growing desire in man for that hazardous day when, without equivocation, he shall establish the sacredness of human life as an inviolable principle. The divine idea is ready for a new incarnation.

Yes, this book will live as a passionate attempt to exalt "the strong upward tendencies and God-like soul of man."

[*November* 20, 1942.]